CONTENTS

Introduction

In the past, achieving crispy, crunchy, and fried flavour that you will love would inevitably need us to deep fry food in oil. This Emeril Lagasse Power Air Fryer 360 has turned the tables. It has replaced the unhealthy oils in food, the mess with cyclonic air that surrounds the food and cooks them to juicy and crispy perfection.

It not only can cook, but also broil, and bake amazing food like French fries, doughnuts, calzones and others. Even better, it has dozens of one-touch preset settings that automatically cook at the ideal temperature and for the ideal time. Don't forget the rotisserie setting that cooks your poultry to perfection in less time than in the oven.

With this life-changing Emeril Lagasse Power Air Fryer 360, you are assured of enjoying the best-tasting main courses, snacks, desserts and others for many years. It's easy to use and easy to clean. I highly recommend this kitchen appliance to every crispy food lover out there.

Chapter 1: Fundamentals Of Emeril Lagasse Power Air Fryer 360

What Is It?

Emeril Lagasse Power Air Fryer 360 is a kitchen appliance that offers you the convenience of the countertop convection oven, air fryer, toaster, slow cooker, dehydrator, and pizza oven all at once. It can roast food for large families and gatherings, dehydrate snacks without preservatives or added sugar, and air fry French fries without oil.

It uses 360°quick-cook technology with five heating elements thus cooking your meals evenly and quickly. Don't forget the display with 12 preset cooking settings including bake, air fry, Dehydrate, rotisserie, warm, reheat, toast, and roast, bagel, broil, pizza, and slow cook. It also has a sleek stainless steel construction that highly complements your kitchen and other appliances in it.

Know About Its Buttons and Functions

Now let's have a look at Emeril Lagasse Power Air Fry 360 preset functions.

Air fry

This is a fast healthy convection cooking method that can be used to replace the messy deep-frying cooking method. Air frying is great for breaded foods with little or no oil. It cooks food by heating from the side heating element and uses the crisper tray in position 4.

Toast

It is used to crisp and brown bread on both sides. It's a great choice for English muffins or loaves of bread. It heats food with both top and bottom heating elements and uses the pizza rack in position 2.

Bagel

It's used to crisp and brown thick bread on both sides. It's also good at toasting bagels, frozen waffles, and rolls. It heats food with both the top and bottom heating elements and uses the pizza rack in position 2.

Pizza

The function is perfect for cooking homemade pizza. It melts the cheese on the top while crisping the dough. It heats food with the top and bottom heating elements and uses the pizza rack in position 5.

Bake

This function is perfect for pastries such as cakes, cookies, pies and others. It cooks the food using the top and bottom elements and the pizza rack in position 5. You can also use the baking tray if you like.

Broil

The broiling function is good for searing a piece of meat, melting cheese on food, and cooks open-face sandwiches. It uses the top heating element and uses the baking pan or the pizza rack in position 1 or 2.

Rotisserie

It's perfect for cooking a whole chicken. The function cooks the food evenly and keeps the food crispy on the outside while juicy on the inside. It uses the top and bottom heating elements and the pizza rack in potion 6.

Slow cook

The function cooks food at low temperatures for longer times. It's perfect for tough meat cuts. It heats food with the top and bottom elements and uses the pizza rack in position 6.

Roast

Perfect for large pieces of poultry and other meat. The function cooks food using the top and bottom elements and uses the pizza rack in position 5.

Dehydrate

Dehydration is perfect for drying fruits, meats, and vegetables. It cooks food in a convection way on low heat. It heats food using the top heating element and uses the crisper tray in positions 1, 4, and 5.

Reheat

The function is used to heat already prepared meals without overcooking them. It uses the top and bottom heating elements to reheat food with the pizza rack in position 5.

Warm

The warm setting holds up food at a safe warm temperature for a certain period of time. It warms food using the top and bottom heating elements and uses the crisper tray, the pizza rack, or the baking pan in potion 5.

It Also Come with Some Knobs and Buttons;

Temperature/ darkness control knob

The knob allows you to adjust the preset temperature and to control the amount of light during toast or bagel.

Time/ slices control knob

The knob allows you to adjust the preset time and also to select the number of slices you want to toast or bagel.

Program selection knob

Allows you to check the preset choices and select one.

Air fry button

Push the button to air fry food or activate the air frying fan for other preset functions.

Light button

Used to light up the interior of the appliance while cooking.

Temperature button

It has°F and°C temperature units and you can choose your preferred method to mature the cooking temperature.

Cancel button

Used to the current cooking process and can power off the unit by pressing it for long.(3 seconds)

Start/ pause button

Starts or pauses the cooking process.

How Does It Work?

The Emeril Lagasse Power Air Fry 360 uses the 360° quick-cook heat technology. This means that you can cook a whole chicken with half an hour less the time you would cook it in a convection oven. The good news is the Emeril Lagasse Power Air Fryer 360 heats up very fast so there's no need to wait until it preheats. You can even cook frozen food directly by just adding a few minutes to the actual cooking time and the food will come out perfectly.

This amazing kitchen appliance comes with a number of accessories. Let's review how they work.

The pizza rack

Insert the drip tray at the very bottom of the appliance then use the markings on the door to place the pizza rack on the ideal position or as recommended on the recipe.

The baking tray

Insert the drip tray at the very bottom of the appliance then use the markings on the door to place the pizza rack as recommended on the recipe. Place the baking pan on the pizza rack and then place the food on the baking tray.

The crisper tray

Insert the drip tray at the very bottom of the appliance then use the markings on the door to place the crisper tray as recommended on the recipe. Place the food on the crisp tray.

The rotisserie spit

Insert the drip tray at the very bottom of the appliance. Remove the forks, and force the rotisserie spit through the food centre lengthwise. Now slide the forks on both sides and tighten them with the set screws. Now insert the rotisserie spit into the rotisserie connections in the appliance. Your food is now ready to be cooked as recommended in the recipe.

Advantages of Using It

1. Using 360°quick-cook turbo heat technology makes it super fast compared to other cooking appliances thus saving on energy and time.
2. Its versatile, and can act as a toaster, dehydrator, rotisserie, slow cooker among others.
3. Easy to clean and maintain. The accessories are dishwasher safe but it is advisable to hand wash them.
4. Very easy to use. With the preset functions, one can easily cook any type of food using the unit.
5. Cooking without oil thus cutting on the intake of calories from oils and fat.

Chapter 2: Tips For Usage, Cleaning, And Maintenance

Tips

1. Cut food into small pieces as it will require less time to cook.
2. Flipping the food halfway through the cooking process ensures even cooked food.
3. Mist a little oil on food.e.g. potatoes or meat for a crispier result.
4. Use pre-made dough instead of homemade dough for quick and easy snacks.
5. You can use a baking dish or a baking tin by placing it on the rack to cook quiches and cakes.

Cleaning and Maintenance

You should clean the Emeril Lagasse Power Air Fryer 360 after every single use.

1. Remove the power cord from the power sauce and ensure the gadget has completely cooled.
2. Use a damp cloth with some mild detergent to wipe the outside.
3. Gently scrub the door with a damp cloth and warm soapy water. The unit should never be soaked in water.
4. Remove any food residue with a nonabrasive brush if it's necessary.
5. Clean the inside with a nonabrasive sponge, hot water, and some mild detergent. Avoid scrubbing the heating elements since they are fragile and may break. Rinse the inside with a clean damp cloth.
6. The accessories should be soaked in warm, soapy water and hand-washed so that the food residue can be easily removed.
7. Make sure that the unit and its components are clean and dry before storing them in a clean and dry place.

Chapter 3: Common Faqs

1.Does Emeril Lagasse Power Air Fryer 360 need time to heat up?
No, the unit has a smart heating feature that heats up the unit to the set temperature before the times start to count down. The smart feature takes effect on all preset settings except dehydrate, bagel, and toast.
2.Is Emeril Lagasse Power Air Fryer 360 healthy?
Yes, Emeril Lagasse Power Air Fryer 360 makes an alternative to your favourite unhealthy fried food using air and not oil. Foods cooked with this unit have about 70% fewer calories compared to the deep-fried food.
3.How much energy does Emeril Lagasse Power Air Fryer 360 consume?
It consumes far less power than other many cooking appliances which saves on energy and money.
4.Do I need to use oil?
No, you don't need oil to get your food crispy. You may, however, spray a little oil to add more flavor.
5.Can I choose my own temperature and time?
Yes, you may manually set the preferred temperature and time as recommended on the recipe instead of using the one-touch preset functions.
6.Can I check my food during the cooking process?
Yes, you just need to press the Start/Pause button to pause the cooking process then open the door. Close the door and press the same button to resume cooking.

Chapter 4: Breakfast Recipes

Omelet in the Emeril Lagasse Power Air Fryer 360

This omelet stuffed with chicken and cheese is more of a lunch than breakfast. It's filling and super delicious.
Prep Time and Cooking Time: 10 minutes| Serves: 2

Ingredients to use:

- 6 eggs
- 3 chicken tenderloins
- 2 slices Harvati cheese
- 1 oz. Butter
- Salsa
- Sour cream

Step-by-step Directions to Cook It:

1. Beat eggs in a mixing bowl.
2. Place the pizza rack at the lowest rack then coat a baking pan with butter.
3. Rotate the Emeril Lagasse Air Fryer 360 temperature knob to 350°F and the timer for 8 minutes. Press the start button to start preheating.
4. Pour egg on the baking pan and place the dish on the rack. After cooking for 4 minutes, pause and spin the pan.
5. Add chicken and cheese then continue to cook for 4 minutes. Fold the omelet over and top with salsa and sour cream.
6. Serve and enjoy.

Nutritional value per serving:

Calories: 479kcal, Carbs: 8g Fat: 32g, Protein: 41g

Basic Omelet

This is one of the easiest recipes you must try in your Emeril Lagasse Power Air Fryer 360. It comes out creamy and fluffy from the inside and surprisingly delicious.
Prep Time and Cooking Time: 50 minutes| Serves: 6

Ingredients to use:

- 10 eggs
- 2 cups of milk
- 1 cup cooked ham, diced
- 1 cup parmesan cheese, grated
- 1/4 cup flat-leaf parsley, freshly chopped
- 1 tbsp. salt
- Black pepper, freshly ground

Step-by-step Directions to Cook It:

1. Grease a baking pan with oil or cooking spray.
2. Beat eggs in a mixing bowl, then whisk in milk. Stir with ham, cheese, and parsley. Season the mixture with salt and pepper.
3. Pour the mixture on the prepared baking dish.
4. Place the baking dish on the pizza rack on position 5 of Emeril Lagasse Air Fryer 360 and select the bake setting. Set the temperature to 375°F and the timer for 45 minutes. Press the start button to start.
5. Insert a knife to test if the omelet is fully cooked.
6. Let rest for 5 minutes before serving.

Nutritional value per serving:

Calories: 313kcal, Carbs: 7.3g Fat: 19.4g, Protein: 26.1g

Baked Eggs

If you're looking for a great way to serve a large crowd with eggs for breakfast, then this is a brilliant way.

Prep Time and Cooking Time: 22 minutes| Serves: 6

Ingredients to use:

- Cooking spray
- 12 eggs
- Salt and pepper

Step-by-step Directions to Cook It:

1. Spray a muffin pan with cooking spray.
2. Crack an egg in each cup and make sure that you don't break the yolk.
3. Place the muffin pan on the pizza rack on position 5 of the Emeril Lagasse Air Fryer 360 and select the bake setting. Set the temperature to 350°F and the timer for 20 minutes. Press the start button to start.
4. Check if the eggs are fully cooked by running the tip of a knife on one egg.
5. Serve immediately after seasoning with salt and pepper.

Nutritional value per serving:

Calories: 150kcal, Carbs: 2g Fat: 10g, Protein: 13g

Baked Eggs with Cheese

This is an amazing simple breakfast recipe that everyone should try out. It comes out so good that everyone will love it and ask for more.

Prep Time and Cooking Time: 23 minutes| Serves: 6

Ingredients to use:

- Cooking spray
- 12 eggs
- 2/3 cup cheese, shredded
- Salt and pepper

Step-by-step Directions to Cook It:

1. Spray a muffin pan with cooking spray.
2. Crack an egg in each cup and make sure that you don't break the yolk. Sprinkle some shredded cheese on each cup.
3. Place the muffin pan on the pizza rack on shelf position 5 of the Emeril Lagasse Air fryer 360 and select the bake setting. Set the temperature to 350°F and the timer for 20 minutes. Press the start button to start.
4. Check if the eggs are fully cooked by running the tip of a knife on one egg. Add more time if not cooked through.
5. Serve immediately when seasoned with salt and pepper.

Nutritional value per serving:

Calories: 200kcal, Carbs: 2g Fat: 6g, Protein: 16g

Sausage and Mushrooms Egg Casserole

Earthy mushrooms and savory sausages are the perfect combinations especially when paired with eggs and some cheese to kick off your day with.

Prep Time and Cooking Time: 55 minutes| Serves: 11

Ingredients to use:

●Cooking spray
●12 oz. breakfast sausage
●1 tbsp. butter
●8 oz. cremini mushrooms, thinly sliced
●12 eggs
●1/2 cup whole milk
●1 tbsp. salt 删去
●1/4 tbsp. black pepper
●8 oz. Havarti cheese, shredded

Step-by-step Directions to Cook It:

1. Spray a baking dish with cooking spray and place two sheets of paper towels on a platter and set aside.
2. Cook sausage on a skillet over medium-high heat for 7 minutes or until browned. Break the sausage into pieces using a rubber spatula.
3. Transfer the cooked sausage to the platter with paper towels.
4. Add butter to the skillet and cook mushrooms for 6 minutes or until the mushrooms have browned and shrunken.
5. Whisk together with eggs, milk, salt, and pepper in a mixing bowl. Add the cooed sausage, mushrooms, and top with cheese. Mix until everything is well distributed.
6. Pour the mixture on the prepared dish and place the dish on the pizza rack of the Emeril Lagasse Air Fryer 360 and press bake.
7. Set the temperature to 350°F and the timer for 40 minutes. Press the start button to start.
8. When the casserole is done, check if it's fully cooked. Cut into squares and spoon on plates. Serve and enjoy.

Nutritional value per serving:

Calories: 100kcal, Carbs: 2g Fat: 7g, Protein: 8g

Sausage and Cheese Egg Casserole

This is a very easy-to-make breakfast casserole that tastes so good that you will want it over and over again.

Prep Time and Cooking Time: 60 minutes| Serves: 10

Ingredients to use:

- Nonstick cooking spray
- 12 oz. breakfast sausage
- 12 eggs
- 1/2 cup whole milk
- 1 tbsp. salt
- 1/4 tbsp. black pepper
- 8 oz. cheddar cheese, shredded

Step-by-step Directions to Cook It:

1. Spray a baking dish with cooking spray and place two sheets of paper towels on a platter and set aside.
2. Cook sausage on a skillet over medium-high heat for 7 minutes or until browned. Break the sausage into pieces using a rubber spatula.
3. Transfer the cooked sausage to the platter with paper towels.
4. Whisk together eggs, milk, salt, and pepper in a mixing bowl. Add the cooked sausage and top with shredded cheese. Mix until everything is well distributed.
5. Pour the mixture on the prepared dish and place the dish on the pizza rack of Emeril Lagasse Air Fryer 360 and press the bake setting.
6. Set the temperature to 350°F and the timer for 45 minutes. Press the start button to start.
7. When the casserole is done, cut into squares and spoon on plates. Serve and enjoy.

Nutritional value per serving:

Calories: 130kcal, Carbs: 1g Fat: 14g, Protein: 14g

Spinach and Artichoke Egg Casserole

This is a perfect meatless breakfast casserole for vegetarians. It's gorgeous, filling, and the best to kick off your morning with.

Prep Time and Cooking Time: 55 minutes| Serves: 11

Ingredients to use:

●Nonstick cooking spray
●1 tbsp. olive oil
●4 oz. baby spinach
●1 can artichoke hertz
●12 eggs
●Scallions, minced
●1/2 cup sour cream
●1/4 tbsp. garlic powder
●1 tbsp. salt
●1/4 tbsp. black pepper
●4 oz. mozzarella cheese, shredded
●4 oz. Italian blend

Step-by-step Directions to Cook It:

1. Spray a baking dish with cooking spray.
2. Heat olive oil in a skillet over medium heat. Add spinach and cook for 2 minutes or until the spinach softens.
3. Add artichoke hertz and cook for 1 more minute. Remove from heat.
4. In a mixing bowl, mix eggs, scallions, sour cream, garlic, salt, and pepper. Add cooked spinach, artichokes, and cheese.
5. Fold until the vegetables are well distributed. Pour the mixture on the baking dish and place the dish on the pizza rack of your Emeril Lagasse Air Fryer 360. Select the bake setting.
6. Set the temperature to 350°F and the timer for 45 minutes. Press the start button to start.
7. When the casserole is done let rest for 10 minutes before serving. Cut into squares and spoon on plates. Serve and enjoy.

Nutritional value per serving:

Calories: 150kcal, Carbs: 2g Fat: 11g, Protein: 10g

Bacon and Cheese Quiche

This quiche is as simple to make as a pie. It's enjoyable both to cook it and eat it. This will be your new favorite.

Prep Time and Cooking Time: 22 minutes| Serves: 6

Ingredients to use:

- 1 pie shell, frozen
- 6 strips of bacon
- 4 eggs
- 3/4 cup whole milk
- 1/4 cup heavy cream
- 1/2 tbsp. salt
- 1/4 tbsp. black pepper
- 2 oz. Gouda cheese, shredded

Step-by-step Directions to Cook It:

1. Poke the pie shell with a fork then place it on a baking sheet.
2. Place the baking sheet on the pizza rack and select bake setting. Set the temperature to 400°F and the timer for 14 minutes. Press the start button to start.
3. Take out from the oven and set aside.
4. Line large dinner plates with paper towels and set aside.
5. Cook bacon on a skillet over medium heat for 8 minutes or until browned and crispy.
6. Transfer the bacon to the lined plates.
7. In a mixing bowl, whisk eggs, milk, heavy cream. Salt and pepper. Add bacon and cheese to the egg mixture and fold until well mixed.
8. Pour the mixture on a pie shell and cover the edges with strips of aluminum foil.
9. Place the pie shell on the pizza rack of the Emeril Lagasse Air Fryer 360 and select the bake setting.
10. Set the temperature to 350°F and the timer for 55 minutes. Press the start button to start.
11. When the quiche is well cooked it should be firm and golden brown. Remove from heat and let rest for 30 minutes before serving. Enjoy.

Nutritional value per serving:

Calories: 210kcal, Carbs: 2g Fat: 18g, Protein: 8g

Baked Potatoes

If you're looking for something new but amazing to serve for breakfast or brunch, then these baked potatoes are a solid choice for you.
Prep Time and Cooking Time: 80 minutes| Serves: 4

Ingredients to use:

- 4 russet potatoes
- 3/4 tbsp. salt
- 1/2 tbsp. black pepper
- 2 scallions, minced
- 1 tbsp. butter
- 4 eggs
- 4 strips bacon
- 1/2 cup cheddar cheese
- Sour cream
- Hot sauce

Step-by-step Directions to Cook It:

1. Line a baking sheet with aluminum foil.
2. Poke each potato 3 times with a fork and wrap with an individual piece of aluminum foil.
3. Place the potatoes on the pizza rack and select bake setting. Set the temperature to 400°F and the timer for 70 minutes. Press the start button to start.
4. Remove potatoes from heat and let them rest to cool. Remove the potatoes from aluminum foil and make a split lengthwise with a knife. Pinch the potatoes to slightly open. Season with salt and pepper.
5. Mince the scallions and melt butter in a skillet over medium heat.
6. In a mixing bowl, crack eggs and whisk until smooth. Add the eggs to the skillet along with half the scallions and half bacon.
7. Cook for 3 minutes while folding. Add half the cheese and fold until it melts. Season with salt and pepper.
8. Place the potatoes on a baking sheet and spoon the egg mixture on them. Sprinkle the remaining cheese on the potatoes.
9. Place the baking sheet on the pizza rack of Emeril Lagasse Air Fryer 360 and select the bake setting.
10. Set the temperature to 400°F and the timer for 10 minutes. Press the start button to start.
11. Sprinkle the remaining scallions and bacon on the potatoes. Serve each potato with sour cream and hot sauce. Enjoy.

Nutritional value per serving:

Calories: 470kcal, Carbs: 40g Fat: 27g, Protein: 18g

Easy Challah French Toast Casserole

This is a perfect crowd pleaser for holiday and gatherings' breakfast. The casserole is yummy and super filling.

Prep Time and Cooking Time: 55 minutes| Serves: 9

Ingredients to use:

- 1 lb. Day-old challah
- 8 eggs
- 1/2 cup of sugar
- 1-7/8 cups whole milk
- 1 tbsp. cinnamon
- 2 tbsp. vanilla extract
- 1/4 tbsp. orange zest
- 1/8 tbsp. salt
- Powdered sugar
- Maple syrup

Step-by-step Directions to Cook It:

1. Spray the casserole dish with cooking spray.
2. Cut the bread into cubes and set aside in a mixing bowl.
3. In a separate mixing bowl, whisk together eggs, sugar, milk, cinnamon, vanilla extract, zest, and salt until well mixed and smooth. Add the bread pieces and fold until well mixed.
4. Pour the mixture into the casserole dish, place the dish on the pizza rack of Emeril Lagasse Air Fryer 360 and select the bake setting. Set the temperature to 400°F and the timer for 50 minutes. Press the start button to start.
5. Let the casserole cool for 30 minutes before serving. Sit sugar and drizzle maple syrup. Enjoy.

Nutritional value per serving:

Calories: 150kcal, Carbs: 18g Fat: 6g, Protein: 7g

Chapter 5: Red Meat Recipes

Blue Cheese Stuffed Burgers

The popular humble hamburger becomes a classic entree when air fried in the Emeril Lagasse Power Air Fryer 360.

Prep Time and Cooking Time: 22 minutes| Serves: 6

Ingredients to use:

- 2 lb. beef, ground
- 2 tbsp. Worcestershire sauce
- 1 tbsp. salt
- 1/2 tbsp. ground black pepper
- 4 slices of bacon, cooked and chopped
- 8 tbsp. crumbled blue cheese
- 1/4 cup butter
- 4 brioche buns
- 8 slices tomato
- 4 Bibb lettuce leaves
- 4 slices red onion

Step-by-step Directions to Cook It:

1. In a mixing bowl, mix beef, sauce, salt, and pepper until well mixed. Make 4 balls from the mixture then divide each ball into a half.
2. Press the ball on a flat surface. Stuff half of it with bacon and 2 tbsp. cheese. Top with the unstuffed meat and seal the edges.
3. Slide the pizza rack on position 2 and place the burgers on the pizza rack.
4. Select the air fry setting of your Emeril Lagasse Air fryer 360 and set the temperature at 400°F for 18 minutes. Press start.
5. Remove the burgers from the rack and set aside to cool. Transfer the pizza rack to position 1 and butter the buns. Place the buns on the rack, butter side up.
6. Select the broil setting. Set temperature at 400°F for 10 minutes. Broil the buns until golden brown.
7. Assemble the buns and burgers with tomatoes, lettuce leaves, and onions.
8. Serve and enjoy.

Nutritional value per serving:

Calories: 590kcal, Carbs: 33g Fat: 35g, Protein: 34g

Air Fid Strip Steak with Red Wine Sauce

This is a delicious steak that is served with wine sauce. The wine sauce makes all the difference, making it a real crowd-pleaser.

Prep Time and Cooking Time: 20 minutes| Serves: 4

Ingredients to use:

●1 lb. strip steak, 1 inch thick
●Salt and pepper
●1 tbsp. butter, unsalted
●1/4 cup shallots, chopped
●1 tbsp. garlic, minced
●1/2 cup dry red wine
●2 tbsp. beef bouillon base
●3 tbsp. heavy cream

Step-by-step Directions to Cook It:

1. Season the steak with salt and pepper and transfer it into the crisper tray. Place the pizza rack on position 1 then place the baking tray on top of it. Place the crisper tray on position 2 of Emeril Lagasse Air Fryer 360.
2. Select the air fry setting. Set the temperature at 400°F for 10 minutes. When the steak is halfway cooked, turn it so that it can be evenly cooked. Let the steak rest for 10 minutes.
3. Meanwhile, prepare the steak. Melt butter in a saucepan over medium heat. Add shallots, garlic, salt, and pepper. Sauté for 1 minute.
4. Add red wine and bring the mixture to boil. Stir with bouillon base until well mixed. Add heavy cream and cook for 1 more minute.
5. Remove the sauce from heat but keep warm.
6. Slice the steak and serve with the sauce.

Nutritional value per serving:

Calories: 649kcal, Carbs: 7.5g Fat: 34g, Protein: 69g

Easy Marinated Steak

This marinated steak is quick to make and very tasty. The liquid smoke gives the steak an addictive flavor that you won't be able to resist.

Prep Time and Cooking Time: 15 minutes| Serves: 2

Ingredients to use:

- 2 8oz Butcher Box New York strip steaks
- 1 tbsp. soy sauce, low sodium
- 1 tbsp. liquid smoke
- 1 tbsp. McCormick's steak seasoning
- 1/2 tbsp. cocoa powder, unsweetened
- Salt and pepper to taste
- Melted butter

Step-by-step Directions to Cook It:

1. Season the steak with soy sauceand liquid smoke until the steak is well seasoned. Refrigerate for a few hours.
2. Place the steak in the crisper tray. Place the pizza rack on position 1 then place the baking tray on top of it. Place the crisper tray on position 2 of your Emeril Lagasse Air Fryer 360.
3. Select the air fry setting and set the temperature at 370°F for 5 minutes.
4. When the steak is well-cooked, with an internal temperature 160°F, remove from heat and serve it with melted butter. Enjoy.

Nutritional value per serving:

Calories: 476kcal, Carbs: 1g Fat: 28g, Protein: 49g

Rib Eye Steak

This is a tender, juicy, and very tasty steak that everyone will love. It's easy to make and can be cooked to your desired level of doneness.

Prep Time and Cooking Time: 22 minutes| Serves: 1

Ingredients to use:

- 16 oz. Rib eye steak
- 1 tbsp. salt
- 3/4 tbsp. pepper
- 1/2 tbsp. garlic powder
- 3/4 steak seasoning

Step-by-step Directions to Cook It:

1. Season the steak with the spices and set aside.
2. Place the steak in the crisper tray. Place the pizza rack on position 1 then place the baking tray on top of it. Place the crisper tray on position 2 of the Emeril Lagasse Air Fryer 360.
3. Select the air fry setting. Set the temperature at 390°F for 12 minutes. Press start.
4. When the steak is halfway cooked, flip it.
5. Transfer the steak to a plate and cover it with a paper foil. Let it rest for 8 minutes before serving it.

Nutritional value per serving:

Calories: 651kcal, Carbs: 7.5g Fat: 49g, Protein: 44g

Steak Bites and Mushrooms

This is an amazing steak with mushrooms that you will love. The good news is that you can use your favorite steak.

Prep Time and Cooking Time: 20 minutes| Serves: 3

Ingredients to use:

- 1 lb. steaks
- 8 oz. mushrooms
- 2 tbsp. butter
- 1 tbsp. Worcestershire sauce
- 1/2 tbsp. garlic powder
- Salt to taste
- Black pepper to taste
- Minced parsley
- Melted butter
- Chili flakes

Step-by-step Directions to Cook It:

1. Pat dry the steak and mushrooms then coat them with butter. Season with Worcestershire sauce, garlic, salt, and pepper.
2. Spread the steak and mushrooms in the crisp tray. Place the pizza rack on position 1 then place the baking tray on top of it. Place the crisper tray on position 2.
3. Select the air fry setting of your Emeril Lagasse Air Fryer 360 then set the temperature at 400°F for 18 minutes.
4. Ensure you shake and flip the steak and mushrooms at least 2 times through the cooking process.
5. Garnish with parsley, butter, and chili flakes.
6. Serve when warm.

Nutritional value per serving:

Calories: 300kcal, Carbs: 2g Fat: 21g, Protein: 24g

Korean Beef Wraps

The homemade Korean beef wrap is as good as the restaurant one. In fact, homemade is more delicious and healthy. Make sure to try it.

Prep Time and Cooking Time: 20 minutes| Serves: 4

Ingredients to use:

- 1/4 cup soy sauce, low sodium
- 2 tbsp. orange juice, fresh
- 1 tbsp. dark brown sugar
- 1 tbsp. red pepper flakes
- 1 tbsp. garlic, minced
- 1 bunch scallions, white part
- 2 tbsp. sesame oil
- 1 lb. sirloin steak
- 2 tbsp. sesame seeds, toasted
- Steamed white rice
- Kimchi
- Romaine Lettuce hearts

Step-by-step Directions to Cook It:

1. In a mixing bowl, mix the first 7 ingredients until well combined. Add the steak and toss to coat well.
2. Let the steak stand for at least 4 hours to marinate.
3. Transfer the steak to the crisper tray. Place the pizza rack on position 1 then place the baking tray on top of it. Place the crisper tray on position 2.
4. Select the air fry setting of your Emeril Lagasse Air Fryer 360 and Set the temperature at 400°F for 10 minutes. Press the start button.
5. When the steak with rice, kimchi wrapped in a lettuce leaf. Enjoy.

Nutritional value per serving:

Calories: 298kcal, Carbs: 11g Fat: 12g, Protein: 35g

Bourbon Rotisserie Roast

Do you love rotisserie roast? I love it. You no longer have to buy it from the store. Make your own at home. It's delicious and the best to serve a crowd.
Prep Time and Cooking Time: 22 minutes| Serves: 6

Ingredients to use:

- 1/2 cup honey
- 1/2 cup light brown sugar
- 1 orange zest
- 2 tbsp. orange juice, fresh
- 1/4 cup bourbon
- 1/2 tbsp. salt
- 1/2 black pepper, ground
- 4 lb. lamb roast

Step-by-step Directions to Cook It:

1. Mix honey, brown sugar, zest, juice, bourbon, salt, and pepper in a mixing bowl.
2. Place the rotisserie spit through the roast and fix the spit with forks.
3. Brush the roast with the marinade until well coated.
4. Place the spit in the Emeril Lagasse Power Air Fryer 360. Select the rotisserie setting and set the temperature at 350°F for 1 hour. Press the start button.
5. Baste the steak with the marinade every 15 minutes and cook until the internal temperature reaches 155°F.
6. Let the meat rest for 15 minutes before serving.

Nutritional value per serving:

Calories: 360kcal, Carbs: 8g Fat: 50g, Protein: 59g

Hanger Steak with Red wine sauce

This steak gives you a met-in-the-mouth experience that you won't be able to resist. It will be your new favorite.

Prep Time and Cooking Time: 25 minutes| Serves: 2

Ingredients to use:

- 2 7oz hanger steaks
- Salt and pepper
- Oil

For the Sauce

- 1 shallot, thinly sliced
- 2 tbsp. butter
- 1 bottle red wine
- 1 cup bee stock
- 1 tbsp. wholegrain mustard

Step-by-step Directions to Cook It:

1. Season the hanger steak with salt and pepper and transfer it into the crisper tray. Place the pizza rack on position 1 then place the baking tray on top of it. Place the crisper tray on position 2.
2. Select the air fry setting on your Emeril Lagasse Air Fryer 360 then set the temperature at 400°F and timer for 10 minutes. When the steak is halfway cooked, turn it so that it can be evenly cooked. Let the steak rest for 10 minutes.
3. Meanwhile, heat a saucepan over medium heat. Cook shallots with butter until translucent. Add wine and cook until almost all the wine has evaporated.
4. Add beef stock and cook until it is reduced by a half.
5. Add mustard and swirl until well combined. Season with salt and pepper to taste.
6. Add a tablespoon of cold butter and swirl the saucepan until it melts. Serve immediately with the hanger steak.

Nutritional value per serving:

Calories: 619kcal, Carbs: 6.5g Fat: 32g, Protein: 63g

Air Fried Beef Tenderloin

Serve your family or friends coming over with this beef tenderloin. It's amazingly crispy on the outside and very juicy from the inside.

Prep Time and Cooking Time: 47 minutes| Serves: 8

Ingredients to use:

- 2 lb. beef tenderloin
- 1 tbsp. vegetable oil
- 1 tbsp. dried oregano
- 1 tbsp. salt
- 1/2 tbsp. black pepper, cracked

Step-by-step Directions to Cook It:

1. Pat dry the tenderloin with a paper towel and place it on a platter.
2. Drizzle vegetable oil and sprinkle oregano, salt, and pepper. Rub the spices on the meat until well coated.
3. Place the roast on the crisper tray. Place the pizza rack on position 1, and then place the baking tray on top of it. Place the crisper tray on position 2.
4. Select the air fry setting. Set temperature at 390°F for 22 minutes. Reduce the temperature to 360°F and cook for 10 minutes.
5. Transfer the meat to a plate and allow to rest while tented with paper foil for 10 minutes before serving.

Nutritional value per serving:

Calories: 235kcal, Carbs: 0.2g Fat: 10.6g, Protein: 32.4g

Air Fried Ground beef

Are you a fan of ground beef? Try this air fried ground beef in the Emeril Lagasse Power air Fryer 360 and you will never make it in the stopover again.
Prep Time and Cooking Time: 12 minutes| Serves: 6

Ingredients to use:

- 1-1/2 lb. ground beef
- 1 tbsp. salt
- 1/2 tbsp. pepper
- 1/2 tbsp. garlic powder

Step-by-step Directions to Cook It:

1. Put the beef in a baking tray then season well with salt, pepper, and garlic powder.
2. Stir well using a wooden spoon.
3. Select the air fry setting on the Emeril Lagasse Air Fryer 360.
4. Set the temperature at 400°F for 5 minutes.
5. Stir well when halfway cooked and continue cooking for the remaining minutes.
6. Crumble the meat well and leave the broth. Use the beef in your favorite recipe.

Nutritional value per serving:

Calories: 134kcal, Carbs: 0.3g Fat: 7.5g, Protein: 15.1g

Chapter 6: Poultry Recipes

Fried Frozen Chicken Tenderloins

Making dinner becomes a snap with these fried chicken tendeloins. They are delicious and a real crowd-pleaser. Your family will ask for more each and every time.

Prep Time and Cooking Time: 30 minutes| Serves: 6

Ingredients to use:

- Southern fried chicken tenderloins

Step-by-step Directions to Cook It:

1. Place the chicken in the crisper tray and place it on the highest rack holder.
2. Select the air fry setting on your Emeril Lagasse Air Fryer 360.
3. Rotate the temperature knob to 425°F and the timer for 25 minutes. Press the start button.
4. Allow the chicken to cook for 15 minutes, then flip and cook for the remaining minutes.
5. Let rest before serving.

Nutritional value per serving:

Calories: 110kcal, Carbs: 0g Fat: 1g, Protein: 13g

Air Fried Chicken Breast

Chicken breasts have a bad reputation for being chewy. Air fried breasts are however surprisingly amazing. They are super crispy on the outside but juicy on the inside.
Prep Time and Cooking Time: 22 minutes| Serves: 6

Ingredients to use:

- 2 chicken breasts, skinless and boneless
- 4 eggs
- 2 cups buttermilk
- 2 cups all-purpose flour
- 2 cups yellow cornmeal
- 1 oz. apple wood smoked salt
- 1 oz. old bay seasoning
- 1 tbsp. black pepper, ground
- Cooking spray

Step-by-step Directions to Cook It:

1. Combine the wet ingredients in a mixing bowl, and then combine the dry ingredients in a separate bowl.
2. Place the pizza rack on position 2 in your Emeril Lagasse Air Fryer 360.
3. Dip each chicken breast in the wet mixture, then in the dry mixture. Spray the chicken with cooking spray and place them on the crisper tray.
4. Place the crisper tray on the level higher than the pizza rack. Select the bake setting. Set the temperature at 425°F for 30 minutes. Press the start button.
5. Check the meat when cooking is complete. The meat should at least have an internal temperature of 165°F.
6. Serve and enjoy.

Nutritional value per serving:

Calories: 188kcal, Carbs: 5g Fat: 6g, Protein: 25g

Rotisserie Chicken

This is an incredible chicken that tastes like a gourmet meal despite minimal preparation and the little hand on time.

Prep Time and Cooking Time: 60 minutes| Serves: 8

Ingredients to use:

●1/4 cup Rustic rub
●4 lb. whole chicken

Step-by-step Directions to Cook It:

1. Rub the chicken with the rustic rub.
2. Fix the rotisserie spit on one side then slide the chicken so the split can run through the chicken. fix the fork and screws.
3. Select the rotisserie setting in the Emeril Lagasse Air Fryer 360. Set the temperature at 350°F for 55 minutes. Press the start button.
4. The chicken should have an internal temperature of 160°F when the cooking cycle is complete. Otherwise, add more minutes.
5. Let the chicken rest for 15 minutes before serving.

Nutritional value per serving:

Calories: 282kcal, Carbs: 0g Fat: 14g, Protein: 44g

Buttermilk Air fried chicken

What is there not to love about buttermilk air fried chicken?. It's the easiest and the healthiest version of the traditional buttermilk chicken.

Prep Time and Cooking Time: 22 minutes| Serves: 6

Ingredients to use:

●2 cups buttermilk
●2 tbsp. salt
●1 tbsp. sugar
●1/2 tbsp. black pepper
●6 chicken legs
●6 chicken thighs
●1cup flour
●6 eggs
●6 cups flaked corn cereal, crushed
●1 tbsp. Emeril Essence seasoning

Step-by-step Directions to Cook It:

1. Pour buttermilk into a mixing bowl then add salt, sugar, and pepper.
2. Soak the chicken pieces in the buttermilk mixture.
3. Add flour in a separate mixing bowl, beat eggs in a separate bowl and add cereal crumbs in a third bowl.
4. Shake the chicken pieces for excess buttermilk and dip them in flour, then in eggs and in crumbs.
5. Place the chicken pieces in the crisper tray. Slide the tray on position 2 of the Emeril Lagasse Air Fryer 360.
6. Select the air fry setting then set the temperature at 375°F for 40 minutes. Press the start button.
7. When the cooking process is complete, the chicken internal temperature should be 160°F.

Nutritional value per serving:

Calories: 335kcal, Carbs: 33.2g Fat: 13g, Protein: 25g

Turkey Meatloaf

This is an amazing solution to sandwiches. It's delicious plus can be made ahead of time and just reheated in the morning.
Prep Time and Cooking Time: 1 hour 15 minutes| Serves: 6

Ingredients to use:

- 1-1/2 lb. ground turkey
- 2/3 cup yellow onion, chopped
- 1/2 cup green bell pepper, chopped
- 1/2 cup dry breadcrumbs, unseasoned
- 1/3 cup celery, chopped
- 1 egg, beaten
- 1/2 cup ketchup
- 1 tbsp. garlic, minced
- 1 tbsp. Emeril original Essence
- 1/2 tbsp. salt
- 1/2 tbsp. black pepper, ground
- 1 tbsp. hot sauce

Step-by-step Directions to Cook It:

1. Place turkey in a mixing bowl. Add yellow onion, green bell pepper, breadcrumbs, celery, egg, 1 tablespoon ketchup, garlic, essence, salt, and black pepper.
2. Mix until well combined. Transfer the mixture to a loaf pan and shape it in a dome shape.
3. Add the remaining ketchup to a small mixing bowl and add the hot sauce. Spoon the mixture on the meatloaf then spread it using the back of the spoon.
4. Place the loaf pan on the pizza rack of the Emeril Lagasse Air Fryer 360 and select bake. Set the temperature at 375°F for 50 minutes. Press start.
5. The meatloaf should have turned golden brown and have an internal temperature of 165°F.
6. Let rest for 5 minutes before serving. Enjoy.

Nutritional value per serving:

Calories: 193kcal, Carbs: 15g Fat: 8g, Protein: 15g

Roasted Turkey Breast with Bacon and Herb Butter

For turkey lovers, roasting turkey breast is much easier than roasting the whole turkey. This is perfect for busy weeknight dinners.

Prep Time and Cooking Time: 1 hour 25 minutes| Serves: 8

Ingredients to use:

- 6 lb. turkey breast, rinsed and dried
- 1 tbsp. salt
- 1 tbsp. black pepper
- 3 tbsp. butter, unsalted
- 1 tbsp. sage leaves, chopped finely
- 1 tbsp. rosemary leaves, chopped finely
- 1 tbsp. oregano leaves, chopped finely
- 1 tbsp. thyme, chopped finely
- 3 bacon slices, cooked and crumbled

Step-by-step Directions to Cook It:

1. Season the turkey breast with salt and pepper on all sides. Transfer them to the crisper tray.
2. Place the crisper tray on the pizza rack. Select the roast setting on Emeril Lagasse Air Fryers 360 and Set temperature at 300°F for 60 minutes. Press start.
3. Reduce heat to 270°F and cook for 15 minutes more or until the internal temperature reaches 165°F.
4. Meanwhile, combine butter, all herbs, bacon, salt, and pepper in a mixing bowl. Refrigerate until ready to use.
5. Serve the turkey with the herb butter.

Nutritional value per serving:

Calories: 336kcal, Carbs: 18g Fat: 8g, Protein: 23g

Pecan Crusted Chicken

These are protein-rich chicken breast coated with pecans making them super crispy, delicious and filling.

Prep Time and Cooking Time: 22 minutes| Serves: 6

Ingredients to use:

- 1 cup pecan pieces
- 1/2 cup breadcrumbs
- 3 tbsp. Creole seasoning
- 2 eggs
- 1/ cup olive oil
- 2 lb. chicken breast, skinless and boneless
- 1/2 cup mayonnaise
- 2 tbsp. honey
- 2 tbsp. Creole mustard
- 1 pinch salt
- 1 pinch cayenne pepper, ground

Step-by-step Directions to Cook It:

1. Combine pecans, breadcrumbs, and 2 tbsp. Creole seasoning in a food processor. Pulse for a minute to mix. Pour the mixture on a dish.
2. In a mixing bowl, beat eggs then add oil, and the remaining Creole.
3. Dip the chicken breast in the egg mixture, then in the pecan mixture shaking to remove excess.
4. Place the chicken on a baking pan. Place the crisper tray on the pizza rack and place the baking pan on top of both.
5. Select air fry setting on Emeril Lagasse Air Fryer 360 and Set temperature at 360°F for 15 minutes. Press start.
6. Meanwhile, mix honey, mustard, salt, and pepper until well combined.
7. Season the chicken breast with salt and pepper during the cooking cycle. Serve with the sauce and enjoy it.

Nutritional value per serving:

Calories: 259kcal, Carbs: 16g Fat: 10g, Protein: 25g

BBQ Cheddar Stuffed Chicken Breasts

Bacon-wrapped chicken breasts are the best. They are classy, delicious, and above all very easy to put together.

Prep Time and Cooking Time: 35 minutes| Serves: 2

Ingredients to use:

- 3 strips bacon
- 2 4oz chicken breast skinless and boneless
- 2 oz. cheddar cheese, cubed
- 1/4 cup BBQ sauce
- 1 pinch o salt and black pepper

Step-by-step Directions to Cook It:

1. Place 1 strip of bacon in a crisper tray and air fry for 2 minutes. Cut the bacon into small pieces.
2. Line the crisper tray with parchment paper.
3. Make a 1 inch cut on the chicken horizontally such that you create an internal pouch.
4. Stuff each chicken breast with cooked bacon and cheese mixture, then wrap the breasts with bacon.
5. Coat the chicken with BBQ sauce and place them on the lined crisper tray. Place the crisper tray on the pizza rack and select air fry.
6. Set temperature of the Emeril Lagasse Power Air Fryer 360 to 380°F and the time for 20 minutes. Press start.
7. Turn the chicken breasts when halfway cooked. The chicken internal temperature should be 165°F when fully cooked. Serve.

Nutritional value per serving:

Calories: 375kcal, Carbs: 12.3g Fat: 19g, Protein: 38g

Sesame Chicken Thighs

These are delicious chicken thighs. Very crispy on the outside and juicy and tender on the inside.
Prep Time and Cooking Time: 55 minutes| Serves: 4

Ingredients to use:

- 2 tbsp. sesame oil
- 2 tbsp. soy sauce
- 1 tbsp. honey
- 1 tbsp. sriracha sauce
- 1 tbsp. rice vinegar
- 2 lb. chicken thighs
- 1 green onion, chopped
- 2 tbsp. sesame seeds, toasted

Step-by-step Directions to Cook It:

1. Combine the first 5 ingredients in a mixing bowl. Add chicken to the bowl and stir until well coated.
2. Cover and refrigerate for at least 30 minutes.
3. Drain the marinade and place the chicken in the crisper tray. Place the crisp tray on the pizza rack of the Emeril Lagasse Power Air Fryer 360.
4. Select the air fry setting and set the temperature at 400°F for 15 minutes. Press start.
5. When you have cooked for 5 minutes, flip and cook for an additional 10 minutes.
6. Let the chicken rest for 5 minutes before serving.

Nutritional value per serving:

Calories: 484kcal, Carbs: 6.6g Fat: 33g, Protein: 40g

Crumbled Chicken Tenderloins

These chicken tenderloins are so simple that you would love to make them over and over again. You can slice chicken breast if you like.

Prep Time and Cooking Time: 27 minutes| Serves: 4

Ingredients to use:

- 1 egg
- 1/2 cup breadcrumbs
- 2 tbsp. vegetable oil
- 8 eaches chicken tenderloins

Step-by-step Directions to Cook It:

1. Whisk the egg in a mixing bowl.
2. Mix bread crumbs and oil in a separate bowl until the mixture is crumbly.
3. Dip each chicken tenderloin in egg then in the crumb mixture until well coated.
4. Lay the tenderloins on the crisper tray and place the tray on the pizza rack.
5. Select air fry on Emeril Lagasse Power Air Fryer 360 and set the temperature at 350°F for 12 minutes. Press start.
6. The internal temperature should be 165°F when the tenderloins are well cooked. Serve and enjoy immediately.

Nutritional value per serving:

Calories: 253kcal, Carbs: 9.8g Fat: 11g, Protein: 26g

Chapter 7: Seafood Recipes

Emeril's Favorite Stuffed Shrimp

This is honestly and truly the perfect way to prepare shrimp in Emeril Lagasse Power Air Fryer 360. The shrimp is delicious, perfect, and full of flavor that your family will love.
Prep time and cook time: 35 minutes| Serves: 6

Ingredients to use:

- 1 tbsp. butter
- 1/2 cup yellow onions, minced
- 1 tbsp. garlic, minced
- 1/4 cup green bell peppers, minced
- 1/2 tbsp. salt
- 1/4 tbsp. black pepper, freshly ground
- 1-1/2 tbsp. hot sauce
- 1 tbsp. Worcestershire sauce
- 3 tbsp. lemon juice, fresh
- 1 lightly beaten egg
- 1/4 cup mayonnaise
- 1/4 cup + 1tbsp. fresh parsley, finely chopped
- 1/4 cup celery, minced
- 2-1/2 tbsp. Creole seasoning
- 1-1/2 cup divided butter crackers, crushed
- 20 shrimps
- 3 tbsp. melted unsalted butter

Step-by-step directions to cook it:

1. Put Sauté butter, onions, garlic, and bell peppers in a sauté pan on a stovetop for about 3 minutes over high-medium heat until soft. Remove from heat and let cool.
2. Once cooled, mix in the remaining ingredients except for 1/4 cup butter crackers, shrimps, and melted butter.
3. Now peel the shrimps except the first-connecting shell segment and tail then devein and butterfly the shrimps lengthwise.
4. Stuff the shrimps with the mixture and splash with melted butter and the remaining crackers.
5. Meanwhile, slide a pizza rack on Emeril Lagasse Power Air Fryer 360 shelf position 1 and crisper tray on shelf position 2. Top the pizza rack with a baking pan.
6. Divide the stuffed shrimps evenly between the baking pan and the crisper tray.
7. Now set the temperature to 400°F and time for 18 minutes then press start.
8. Serve with lemon wedges. Enjoy!

Nutritional Value per Serving:

calories: 352Kcal, Carbs: 5.4g, Fat: 36.8g, Protein: 1.8g

Rosemary and Salted Roasted Shrimp with Garlic Butter Dipping Sauce

This roasted shrimp has a very unique sweetness. It is very easy for beginners using Emeril Lagasse Power Air Fryer 360 and everyone including your visitors will be left asking for more.
Prep time and cook time: 1 hour 15 minutes| Serves: 4

Ingredients to use:

- 3-4 lbs. rock salt
- 8 fresh rosemary sprigs, halved and 1/4 tbsp. minced leaves
- 20 shrimps, large and shell on
- 1 unsalted butter stick
- 1 tbsp. garlic, chopped
- 1 tbsp. lemon juice
- 1/4 tbsp. salt
- 1/8 tbsp. red pepper flakes

Step-by-step directions to cook it:

1. Set your Emeril Lagasse Power Air Fryer 360 at 400°F and to roast setting.
2. Spread about 1/4 of rock salt at the bottom of a baking sheet making an even layer then preheat in an oven for about 30-45 minutes.
3. Place rosemary sprigs evenly on hot salt. Then place 1 shrimp over each rosemary sprig then cover completely with the remaining rock salt.
4. Roast for about 10-12 minutes until cooked through and shrimps are pink. Repeat for the remaining shrimps.
5. In the meantime, melt butter in a small saucepan over medium heat then add all the remaining ingredients. Cook gently for 5 minutes until fragrant.
6. Remove from heat and transfer into a decorative bowl.
7. Serve shrimps with butter dipping sauce. Serve warm.

Nutritional Value per Serving:

Calories: 345Kcal, Carbs: 4g, Fat: 25.2g, Protein: 25.6g

Crispy Air Fried Shrimp Sliders

This recipe is great when prepared in your home. These crispy air fried shrimp sliders may become the family's favorite and everyone will love it.
Prep time and cook time: 45 minutes| Serves: 6

Ingredients to use:

- 3/4 lb. chopped shrimp, peeled and deveined
- 2 tbsp. red bell pepper, minced
- 1/4 cup yellow onion, finely chopped
- 1/2 large beaten egg
- 1/4 cup celery, finely chopped
- 1 tbsp. Creole seasoning
- 1/8 tbsp. cayenne
- 1/8 tbsp. salt
- 2 tbsp. green onions, finely chopped
- 1/2 tbsp. baking powder
- 2 tbsp. flat-leaf parsley, chopped
- 8 tbsp. breadcrumbs
- 1/2 minced Serrano pepper
- Cooking spray, nonstick
- For serving: slider buns
- Optional: lettuce leaves, tomato slices, tartar sauce

Step-by-step directions to cook it:

1. Combine shrimps, bell pepper, onion, egg, and celery in a bowl.
2. Add Creole seasoning, cayenne, salt, green onions, baking powder, parsley, and 2 tbsp. bread crumbs and mix everything well.
3. Cover the mixture and refrigerate for about 2 hours.
4. Remove from the refrigerator and divide it into 6 patties about 1/3 cup measures each.
5. Dredge the patties gently in the remaining breadcrumbs and coat all sides lightly.
6. Preheat Emeril Lagasse Power Air Fryer 360 at 400°F and set the timer to 18 minutes then spray the baking tray with the cooking spray.
7. Place the patties on the baking tray and spray each patty top with cooking spray.
8. Place the tray into your air fryer and cook for about 16-18 minutes until crispy and golden.
9. Serve with slider buns, lettuce leaves, tomato slices, and tartar sauce.

Nutritional Value Per Serving:

Calories: 125Kcal, Carbs: 11.2g, Fat: 1.9g, Protein: 15.2g

Snapper Fillets Baked in a Creole Sauce

This is a seafood recipe that your family can have at any time without anyone complaining. It is healthy, nourishing, and comforting.
Prep time and cook time: 45 minutes| Serves: 4

Ingredients to use:

- 2 lb. red snapper fillets, scales, and pin bones removed
- 1 tbsp. cayenne pepper
- 1 tbsp. kosher salt
- 4 tbsp. unsalted butter
- 2-1/2 cups yellow onions, chopped
- 3/4 cup celery, chopped
- 3/4 cup green bell peppers, chopped
- 3 bay leaves
- 2 fresh thyme sprigs
- 1 tbsp. garlic, chopped
- 1/2 cup green onions, chopped
- 2 tbsp. all-purpose flour, bleached
- 2 cups tomatoes, chopped and seeded
- 1 tbsp. Worcestershire sauce
- 2 cups chicken stock
- 1 tbsp. hot sauce
- For garnish: chopped parsley

Step-by-step directions to cook it:

1. Season the fillets with 1/2 tbsp. cayenne pepper and 2 tbsp. salt then refrigerate.
2. Melt butter in a stockpot over high-medium heat.
3. Add onions, celery, bell peppers, the remaining salt, the remaining cayenne, bay leaves, and thyme.
4. Cook for about 10 minutes until onions are golden and soft. Stir often.
5. Stir with garlic and green onions then for about 1 minute until fragrant.
6. Stir with flour and cook for about 2 minutes. While stirring, do not brown the flour.
7. Add tomatoes, Worcestershire, chicken stock, and pepper sauce then cook for about 10 minutes over medium heat.
8. Add parsley, remove sauce from heat and cool for about 15 minutes.
9. Preheat Emeril Lagasse Power Air Fryer 360 to 325°F.
10. Butter your casserole dish then pour the sauce in. Nestle the fillets in the sauce and bake for about 35 minutes until cooked through and flesh is firm.
11. Serve with warm bread.

Nutritional Value Per Serving:

Calories: 581Kcal, Carbs: 42.2g, Fat: 16.8g, Protein: 65.8g

Baked Mushrooms Stuffed with Crabmeat Imperial

Looking for a delicious seafood recipe prepared in an Emeril Lagasse Power Air Fryer 360? Baked Mushrooms Stuffed with Crabmeat Imperial is what you are looking for. It is delicious every time.

Prep time and cook time: 25 minutes| Serves: 6-8

Ingredients to use:

- 1 cup mayonnaise
- 1 tbsp. lemon juice, fresh
- 1 tbsp. Dijon mustard
- 1/2 tbsp. Worcestershire sauce
- 1/2 tbsp. hot red pepper sauce
- 1/8 tbsp. cayenne
- 1/4 tbsp. salt
- 1 tbsp. butter
- 1/4 cup yellow bell pepper, finely chopped
- 1/4 cup red onions, finely chopped
- 1/4 cup celery, finely chopped
- 1 tbsp. minced garlic
- 2 tbsp. green onions, minced
- 1 tbsp. fresh dill, minced
- 1 tbsp. fresh parsley, minced
- 1 lb. lump crabmeat, cartilage removed
- 1/4 - 1/2 cup parmesan, grated
- For garnish: fresh chives
- 36 cremini mushrooms, stems removed and wiped clean

Step-by-step directions to cook it:

1. Preheat Emeril Lagasse Power Air Fryer 360 to 400°F.
2. Combine mayonnaise, lemon juice, mustard, Worcestershire sauce, pepper sauce, cayenne, and salt in a large bowl, then stir to blend well. Set aside.
3. Melt butter in a skillet, medium, over high-medium heat.
4. Add bell peppers, red onions, and celery. Cook and stir for about 2 minutes until soft.
5. Add garlic and green onions then cook for 30 seconds while stirring. Remove from heat and cool.
6. Now add mayonnaise mixture, dill, and parsley. Stir to blend well.
7. Fold in crab meat gently.
8. Stuff each mushroom with crabmeat imperial mixture, place on a baking sheet, and splash with parmesan cheese.
9. Bake on shelf 5 for about 8-10 minutes until meat is bubbly and warmed through.
10. Transfer from the oven to a platter then garnish with chives.
11. Serve and enjoy.

Nutritional Value Per Serving:

Calories: 254Kcal, Carbs: 11.9g, Fat: 15.2g, Protein: 17.5g

Crabmeat Imperial

Do you need a family pleaser? Crabmeat Imperial is a perfect, healthy, and an excellent recipe that your family including your kids will love.
Prep time and cook time: 25 minutes| Serves:4

Ingredients to use:

- 1 tbsp. olive oil
- 3/4 cup yellow onions, small and diced
- 1/4 cup red peppers, small and diced
- 2 tbsp. shallots, minced
- 1/4 cup celery, small and diced
- 1/4 tbsp. cayenne
- 3/4 tbsp. salt
- 1 lb. crab meat
- 2 tbsp. parsley, chopped
- 1 tbsp. minced garlic
- 1/4 cup green onions, chopped
- 1 cup mayonnaise, homemade
- 1/4 tbsp. Tabasco
- 2 tbsp. Creole mustard
- 1/4 cup fine bread crumbs, dried
- 1/2 tbsp. Creole seasoning
- For garnish: 2 tbsp. chives, chopped

Step-by-step directions to cook it:

1. Heat oil in a large sauté pan, and then add onions, peppers, shallots, celery, cayenne, and salt. Sauté for about 5 minutes until soft.
2. Add crab meat, parsley, garlic, and green onions. Sauté for another 1-2 minutes.
3. Remove from heat then cool for 30 minutes.
4. Once cooled, combine the mixture with 3/4cup mayonnaise, Tabasco, and mustard mixing thoroughly until well mixed. Scoop the mixture into a ramekin, medium-sized.
5. Combine the remaining mayonnaise, bread crumbs, and rustic rub. Spread the mixture over the crab mixture.
6. Place a tray on shelf position 2 in your Emeril Lagasse Power Air Fryer 360 to 400°F. Select the bake setting and set the timer for 6 minutes.
7. Press the start button. Cook until crab meat is brown and bubbly.
8. Transfer onto a platter and garnish with chives.
9. Serve with crackers.

Nutritional Value Per Serving:

Calories: 430Kcal, Carbs: 27.1g, Fat: 26.5g, Protein: 16.7g

Tuna Steak

This is a fancy and perfect way to impress your guests and your kids. This tuna steak is a recipe that when prepared in an Emeril Lagasse Power Air Fryer 360, everyone will be left asking for more.

Prep time and cook time: 25 minutes| Serves: 2

Ingredients to use:

- 1/2 lb. tuna steak
- Sea salt, smoked
- Black pepper, freshly ground
- Old bay seasoning

Step-by-step directions to cook it:

1. Season tuna steak with salt, pepper , and seasoning to taste. Place it on a baking pan.
2. Place pizza rack on shelf position 2, select roast setting on your Emeril Lagasse Power Air Fryer 360 preheated to 355°F , and set the timer to 17 minutes.
3. Place the baking pan on the pizza rack, close the air fryer, and press the start button.
4. Cook until the steak temperature is 145°F.
5. Serve and enjoy.

Nutritional Value Per Serving:

Calories: 217Kcal, Carbs: 2.1g, Fat: 7.2g, Protein: 34.3g

Whole Salmon Fillet

This recipe is perfect for beginners as it is easy, quick to cook, and delicious. Salmon fillet requires a few minutes thus perfect for a person who hates rushing in getting meals ready. you won't regret it.

Prep time and cook time: 35 minutes| Serves: 4

Ingredients to use:

●3 lb. salmon fillet, halved
●Sea salt, smoked
●Black pepper, freshly ground
●Old bay seasoning

Step-by-step directions to cook it:

1. Season the salmon halves with salt, pepper, and seasonings.
2. Lines a convection safe grill on 2 crisper trays then place the salmon halves into the trays.
3. Select roast setting with your Emeril Lagasse Power Air Fryer 360 preheated to 355°F, and set the timer to 30 minutes.
4. Place 1 crisper tray on shelf position 1 and the other on shelf position 2.
5. Close the air fryer and press the start button.
6. Cook until the salmon temperature is 145°F.
7. Serve and enjoy.

Nutritional Value per Serving:

Calories: 454Kcal, Carbs: 1g, Fat: 21.1g, Protein: 66.2g

Seafood Tacos

These seafood tacos are fast, easy, and delicious. It is best prepared using Emeril Lagasse Power Air Fryer 360 which makes you feel confident as a beginner. You will love it.
Prep time and cook time: 25 minutes| Serves: 10

Ingredients to use:

- 2, 8-oz, bags mesquite barbecue potato chips
- 1 cup flour
- 1/8 cup buttermilk
- 4 eggs
- 20 deveined shrimps, peeled and tail removed
- 2 lb. flounder pieces
- 1 lb. diced tomatoes
- 2 Corn kernels
- 1/2 diced red onion
- 6 diced jalapenos, seeded
- 1/2 diced orange pepper
- 1 tbsp. chili powder
- 1 lime juice
- 1/2 tbsp. ancho chili powder
- 1/16 tbsp. cumin
- 1/8 tbsp. cayenne powder, ground
- 1/2 cup grape seed oil
- 1/2 cup sour cream
- 2 tbsp. cilantro leaves, chopped
- 6 minced Serrano peppers
- 1 tbsp. lime juice, fresh
- 1/16 tbsp. black pepper, ground
- 1/16 tbsp. salt
- 20 flour tortillas
- 3 avocados, sliced
- 2 wedged limes

Step-by-step directions to cook it:

1. Process and crush barbeque chips in a food processor.
2. Place flour in a baking dish, shallow.
3. Place buttermilk and eggs in another dish. Beat the eggs using a fork.
4. Place the crushed chips in a third dish.
5. Now dredge the shrimps and flounder in the flour, then buttermilk mixture, and lastly in the chips.
6. Place shrimp and flounder on a crisper tray and place the tray on shelf position 2.
7. Select the air-fry setting on the Emeril Lagasse Power Air Fryer 360 and set the temperature at 400°F, and timer to 18 minutes. Press the start button to begin cooking.
8. Meanwhile, combine tomatoes, corn kernels, red onion, jalapenos, orange pepper, chili powder, lime juice, Ancho chili powder, cumin, cayenne pepper, and oil in a large bowl. This is corn-tomato salsa.
9. Combine sour cream, cilantro leaves, Serrano peppers, lime juice, pepper, and salt in another bowl. This is Serrano crema.
10. Remove shrimp and fish from the fryer and serve with corn-tomato salsa, serrano crema, avocado slices, lime wedges, and tortillas.
11. Enjoy.

Nutritional Value Per Serving:

Calories: 721Kcal, Carbs: 73.5g, Fat: 29.2g, Protein: 43.9g

Roasted Salmon

Roasted salmon comes with a wonderful taste when prepared in an Emeril Lagasse Power Air Fryer 360. It is a recipe to have at any time.

Prep time and cook time: 25 minutes| Serves: 4

Ingredients to use:

- 2 lb. salmon fillet
- 1 tbsp. lemon juice, fresh
- 2 tbsp. Emeril's Essence seasoning

Step-by-step directions to cook it:

1. Place the fillet on a baking dish then season with seasoning and lemon juice.
2. Place a pizza rack on shelf position 1 in your Emeril Lagasse Power Air Fryer 360 then place the pan on the pizza rack.
3. Select roast settings on the Emeril Lagasse Power Air Fryer 360 and set the temperature at 350°F, and set time for 20 minutes.
4. Press the start button.
5. Serve and enjoy.

Nutritional Value Per Serving:

Calories: 301Kcal, Carbs: o.1g, Fat: 14g, Protein: 44g

Chapter 8: Vegetarian Recipes

Sicilian Style Air Fried Broccoli

If you are a lover of roasted broccoli, then this air fried version will excite you. Very crispy and tender , making a perfect quick sandwich.
Prep Time and Cooking Time: 30 minutes| Serves: 4

Ingredients to use:

- 1-1/2 lb. broccoli florets, trimmed
- 1/2 tbsp. sea salt or more to taste
- 3 tbsp. olive oil
- 1/2 onion, julienned
- 1 tbsp. garlic, minced
- 1/2 tbsp. red pepper, crushed
- 1/4 cup kalamata olives, chopped
- 2 anchovy fillets, chopped
- 1 tbsp. nonpareil capers, drained
- 1 lemon zested and juiced
- 1/3 cup golden raisins
- 2 tbsp. parmesan cheese

Step-by-step Directions to Cook It:

1. Add water to a saucepan up to three-quarters full and bring to boil over high heat.
2. Add broccoli and cook for 2 minutes. Drain the broccoli and transfer them to a mixing bowl.
3. Toss broccoli with oil, onion, garlic, salt, and pepper.
4. Place half of the broccoli florets onto a baking tray and slide it in position 5.
5. Select roast setting on the Emeril Lagasse Power Air Fryer 360 and set the temperature at 425°F for 12 minutes. Press start.
6. Cook until the broccoli is tender and the onions are slightly golden brown. Transfer them to a serving bowl then cook the remaining batch.
7. Add kalamata olives, anchovies, capers, lemon juice, and raisins to the broccoli. Adjust seasoning to your liking.
8. Garnish with zest, cheese, and pepper. Serve when warm.

Nutritional value per serving:

Calories: 43kcal, Carbs: 8g Fat: 1g, Protein: 3g

Zucchini, Yellow Squash and Carrots

This is an amazing way to add vegetables to your meals. The veggies are super delicious when served as a side of your likings.

Prep Time and Cooking Time: 45 minutes| Serves: 4

Ingredients to use:

- 1/2 lb. carrots, peeled and cut into cubes
- 6 tbsp. olive oil
- 1 lb. zucchini stems and roots trimmed
- 1 lb. yellow squash stems and roots trimmed
- 1 tbsp. salt
- 1/2 tbsp. white pepper, ground
- 1 tbsp. tarragon leaves, chopped

Step-by-step Directions to Cook It:

1. In a mixing bowl, combine carrots and 2 tbsp. oil. Toss until well combined.
2. Place the carrots on a crisper tray. Slide it on position 2 of the Emeril Lagasse Power Air Fryer 360 and select the air fry setting. Set the temperature at 400°F for 5 minutes. Press start.
3. Meanwhile, place zucchini and squash in a mixing bowl. Drizzle the remaining oil salt and pepper. Toss well to coat.
4. Add the zucchini and squash to the crisper tray with carrots. Add 30 more minutes. The vegetables should be fully cooked and browned.
5. Toss the vegetables with tarragon and serve while warm.

Nutritional value per serving:

Calories: 128kcal, Carbs: 16g Fat: 7.2g, Protein: 2.5g

Air Fried Asparagus

With only three ingredients, asparagus will become your favorite vegetarian dish. It's a very healthy and easy side dish that everyone one will love.

Prep Time and Cooking Time: 10 minutes| Serves: 2

Ingredients to use:

●1 bunch asparagus, woody ends trimmed
●Olive oil
●Bragg nutritional yeast

Step-by-step Directions to Cook It:

1. Thoroughly wash asparagus.
2. Spay the asparagus stalks with oil then sprinkle the yeast.
3. Lay the asparagus in a semi single layer on the crisper tray. Slide the tray on position 2.
4. Select the air fry setting on the Emeril Lagasse Power Air Fryer 360 and set the temperature at 360°F for 8 minutes. Press start.
5. Serve when warm with your favorite sauce.

Nutritional value per serving:

Calories: 118kcal, Carbs: 10.3g Fat: 8.1g, Protein: 5.2g

Air Fried Green Beans with Shallots and Almonds

You should definitely add these air fried green beans with shallots and almonds to your Thanksgiving menu. These green beans will amaze you with their goodness.

Prep Time and Cooking Time: 25 minutes| Serves: 4

Ingredients to use:

- 1-1/2 lb. green beans, stems removed
- 2 tbsp. salt
- 1/2 lb. shallots, peeled and stem removed
- 1/2 tbsp. white pepper
- 2 tbsp. olive oil
- 1/4 cup slivered almonds, toasted lightly

Step-by-step Directions to Cook It:

1. Add water to a saucepan up to three-quarters full. Bring to boil then add green beans with a tablespoon salt. Cook for 2 minutes.
2. Drain the beans on a colander and place them in a mixing bowl. Add shallots, a tablespoon salt, pepper, and olive oil. Toss until well combined.
3. Place them on the crisper tray and slide it on position 2 of the Emeril Lagasse Power Air Fryer 360.
4. Select air fry and set the temperature at 400°F for 25 minutes. Press start.
5. Toss them frequently while cooking.
6. Serve the green beans when hot. Enjoy.

Nutritional value per serving:

Calories: 164kcal, Carbs: 12.2g Fat: 10g, Protein: 5g

Honey Butter Glazed Carrots

These honey butter glazed carrots are incredibly delicious. The little garlic plus olive oil just takes the carrots to a higher level.
Prep Time and Cooking Time: 35 minutes| Serves: 4

Ingredients to use:

- 8 carrots, rainbow-colored, peeled and sliced
- 4 tbsp. butter
- 1/4 cup vegetable stock
- 1 tbsp. lemon juice
- 2 sprigs rosemary
- 2 tbsp. raw honey
- Salt and pepper

Step-by-step Directions to Cook It:

1. Place the carrots, butter, vegetable stock, lemon juice, and rosemary in a pan of the Emeril Lagasse Power Air Fryer 360.
2. Select air fry and set the temperature at 320°F for 20 minutes. Press start.
3. When the time has elapsed, add honey and cook for 15 more minutes while stirring every 7 minutes.
4. Serve when hot.

Nutritional value per serving:

Calories: 79kcal, Carbs: 12.3g Fat: 2.9g, Protein: 0.2g

Green Beans with Garlic Lime Dip

Prep Time and Cooking Time: 15 minutes| Serves: 2

Ingredients to use:

- 1/2 cup flour
- 2 eggs
- 1 cup plain breadcrumbs
- 2 tbsp. blackening spice
- 1 lb. green beans
- 1 cup mayonnaise
- 1 garlic clove
- 1/2 lime juice
- 2 tbsp. parsley

Step-by-step Directions to Cook It:

1. Pour flour into a mixing bowl.
2. Beat egg in another bowl and mix breadcrumbs mixture ingredients in another bowl.
3. Dredge green beans in flour, then in eggs, and finally in the breadcrumbs.
4. Place the green beans on the crisper tray and place it on position 2 of the Emeril Lagasse Power Air Fryer 360. Select air fry.
5. Set the temperature at 400°F for 10 minutes. Press start. Rotate the tray when halfway cooked.
6. Combine the dip ingredients in a mixing bowl. Serve the dip with green beans when warm.

Nutritional value per serving:

Calories: 150kcal, Carbs: 2g Fat: 10g, Protein: 13g

Wedged Potatoes

If you are a French fries lover but want to keep it healthy, these potato wedges are a great choice for you.

Prep Time and Cooking Time: 20 minutes| Serves: 6

Ingredients to use:

- 4 Russet potatoes washed and wedged
- 2 tbsp. olive oil
- 2 tbsp. Emeril's Essence seasoning

Step-by-step Directions to Cook It:

1. Toss the potatoes in oil and sprinkle the seasoning.
2. Arrange the potatoes on the crisper tray then slide the tray on shelf position 2 of the Emeril Lagasse Power Air Fryer 360. Select the air fry setting.
3. Set the temperature at 400°F for 18 minutes. Press start.
4. Remove the potato wedges from the crisper tray and serve with steak. Enjoy.

Nutritional value per serving:

Calories: 240kcal, Carbs: 27g Fat: 4.5g, Protein: 3g

Dehydrated Onions

Onions are super easy to dehydrate. Dehydrated onions are immensely versatile and take less storage space compared to fresh onions.

Prep Time and Cooking Time: 10 hours| Serves: 4

Ingredients to use:

- 2 white onions, sliced into 1/4 inches thick

Step-by-step Directions to Cook It:

1. Cut the white onions into rings.
2. Arrange the rings on the crisper tray and slide the tray on shelf position 2 on top of the pizza rack of the Emeril Lagasse Power Air Fryer 360.
3. Select the dehydrate setting. Set the temperature at 120°F for 10 hours. Press start.
4. Cook until the onions are crispy.

Nutritional value per serving:

Calories: 17kcal, Carbs: 4.1g Fat: 0.02g, Protein: 0.5g

Roasted Vegetables

These roasted vegetables are an amazing side dish for everyone. They are easy to prepare and in fact, can be made ahead of time.
Prep Time and Cooking Time: 55 minutes| Serves: 6

Ingredients to use:

- 1 butternut squash, cubed
- 2 red bell peppers, seeded and diced
- 1 sweet potato
- 3 Yukon Gold potatoes, cubed
- 1 red onion, quartered
- 1 tbsp. fresh thyme, chopped
- 2 tbsp. fresh rosemary, chopped
- 1/4 cup olive oil
- 2 tbsp. balsamic vinegar
- Salt and pepper to taste

Step-by-step Directions to Cook It:

1. In a mixing bowl, mix butternut squash, bell pepper, sweet potato, and potatoes. Cut the onion into quarters and add to the squash mixture.
2. Mix in thyme, rosemary, oil, vinegar, salt, and pepper. Toss the vegetables until well coated with oil.
3. Spread the vegetables on a pan and slide the pan on shelf position 2 of the Emeril Lagasse Power Air Fryer 360 over the pizza rack.
4. Select roast setting. Set the temperature at 475°F for 40 minutes. Press start.
5. The vegetables should be cooked through and browned. Serve.

Nutritional value per serving:

Calories: 123kcal, Carbs: 20g Fat: 4.7g, Protein: 2g

Roasted Squash with Crushed Pistachios

This butternut squash is roasted until caramelized and scattered with pistachios as an amazing side dish.

Prep Time and Cooking Time: 50 minutes| Serves: 4

Ingredients to use:

- 1 butternut squash, peeled and cut into cubes
- 2 tbsp. olive oil
- Salt and pepper
- 50g pistachios, toasted
- 4 sprigs of thyme, leaves
- 1 lemon juice

Step-by-step Directions to Cook It:

1. Toss butternut squash with oil and season with salt and pepper.
2. Place the squash on a pan and place the pan on the pizza tray of the Emeril Lagasse Power Air Fryer 360.
3. Select roast setting. Set the temperature at 400°F for 40 minutes. Press start.
4. Cook the onions until caramelized and tender.
5. Meanwhile, crush the pistachios, thyme, and salt in a bowl. Stir with lemon juice and adjust seasoning if you like.
6. Spoon the pistachios over squash and enjoy.

Nutritional value per serving:

Calories: 209kcal, Carbs: 19g Fat: 11g, Protein: 5g

Chapter 9: Bread, Bagel, And Pizza

Cheddar Jalapeno Cornbread

This is a delicious bread to serve for breakfast. It has a super moist crumb and crispy edges on top that are spicy and cheesy.
Prep Time and Cooking Time: 40 minutes| Serves: 6

Ingredients to use:

- 1-1/2 cup all-purpose flour
- 1-1/2 cup yellow cornmeal
- 1-1/5 tbsp. baking powder
- 1-1/2 tbsp. salt
- 1-1/2 cup whole milk
- 1/4 tbsp. cayenne pepper, ground
- 3 eggs
- 1/2 cup sharp cheddar
- 1-1/2 tbsp. green jalapeno, minced
- 1-1/2 tbsp. red jalapeno, minced
- 1/3 cup vegetable oil plus 1 tbsp. vegetable oil
- 1-1/2 tbsp. honey
- 1/2 tbsp. butter

Step-by-step Directions to Cook It:

1. In a mixing bowl, mix flour, cornmeal, baking powder, salt, and pepper until well combined.
2. In another bowl, mix milk, eggs, cheese, jalapenos, and 1/3 cup vegetable oil.
3. Mix the dry ingredients into the wet ingredients. Grease a baking pan with the remaining oil and pour the mixture.
4. Slide the pizza rack on shelf position 5 of the Emeril Lagasse Power Air Fryer 360 and place the baking pan on top.
5. Select the bake setting. Set the temperature at 325°F for 30 minutes. Press start.
6. Cook until the toothpick comes out clean when inserted in the bread.
7. Brush the bread with honey and butter, then let rest to cool before serving.

Nutritional value per serving:

Calories: 201kcal, Carbs: 27g Fat: 8.2g, Protein: 6g

Family Banana Nut Bread

This banana nut bread is just incredible. It's easy to make and the best breakfast to kick off the day with.

Prep Time and Cooking Time: 1 hour 15 minutes| Serves: 10

Ingredients to use:

- 8 oz. cream cheese, softened
- 1 cup white sugar
- 1/2 cup butter
- 2 eggs, beaten
- 2 ripe bananas, mashed
- 2-1/4 cups all-purpose flour
- 1/2 tbsp. baking soda
- 1-1/2 tbsp. baking powder
- 1 cup walnuts, chopped

Step-by-step Directions to Cook It:

1. Beat cream cheese, sugar, butter, eggs, and mashed banana in a mixing bowl until well mixed and smooth.
2. Stir with flour, baking soda, baking powder, and walnuts until well combined. Pour the batter on a greased loaf pan.
3. Slide the pizza rack on shelf position 5 and place the loaf pan on top.
4. Select the bake setting on the Emeril Lagasse Power Air Fryer 360 and set the temperature at 350°F for 75 minutes. Press start
5. Let the bread cool for 10 minutes before serving.

Nutritional value per serving:

Calories: 449kcal, Carbs: 49.3g Fat: 26g, Protein: 8g

Basic Fruit Bread

This fruit bread is super versatile. You can use any fruit, nuts, vegetables, spices or your favorite combination.

Prep Time and Cooking Time: 50 minutes| Serves: 6

Ingredients to use:

- 3 cups all-purpose flour
- 2 tbsp. baking powder
- 1 tbsp. baking soda
- 1/2 tbsp. salt
- 1 cup white sugar
- 1/2 cup vegetable oil
- 2 eggs
- 1 cup apple, shredded
- 3/4 cup walnuts, chopped
- 1/2 tbsp. vanilla extract

Step-by-step Directions to Cook It:

1. In a mixing bowl, mix flour, baking powder, baking soda, salt, white sugar, vegetable oil, eggs, apple, walnuts, and vanilla extract until moistened
2. Grease the loaf pan and pour the mixture on it.
3. Slide the pizza rack on shelf position 5 of the Emeril Lagasse Power Air Fryer 360 and place the loaf pan on top.
4. Select the bake setting. Set the temperature at 350°F for 35 minutes. Press start.
5. Let the bread cool before serving.

Nutritional value per serving:

Calories: 391kcal, Carbs: 52g Fat: 18g, Protein: 7g

Mini Pizza with Italian Sausage

Pizza is popular for parties or day outs. The good news is you can now make your own pizza at home and eat as much as you can. In fact, homemade is more customized and delicious than a store-bought pizza.

Prep Time and Cooking Time: 50 minutes| Serves: 4

Ingredients to use:

- 1 lb. pizza dough
- 1-1/2 lb. Hot Italian Sausage
- 3-1/2 tomato sauce
- 8 oz. mozzarella cheese
- 2 tbsp. thyme leaves, freshly chopped
- 1/2 tbsp. red pepper, crushed
- 1/4 cup Parmigiano-Reggiano, finely grated
- Extra virgin oil

Step-by-step Directions to Cook It:

1. Divide the dough into 4 portions on a work surface with flour. Roll each dough on the work surface into an 8 inches round.
2. Place the sausage on the crisper tray and slide the tray on position 2 of the Emeril Lagasse Power Air Fryer 360.
3. Select the air fry setting and set the temperature at 400°F for 15 minutes. Press start.
4. Transfer the dough to the crisper tray and spoon the tomato sauce on each dough surface. Sprinkle cheese, top with the sausage, and garnish with thyme, pepper, and Parmigiano-Reggiano.
5. Slide the crisper tray on shelf position 2. Select the pizza setting. Set the temperature at 425°F for 20 minutes. Press start.
6. Repeat the cycle with the remaining 3 pizzas. Serve the pizza drizzled with olive oil.

Nutritional value per serving:

Calories: 130kcal, Carbs: 13g Fat: 5g, Protein: 6g

Roasted Garlic Pizza with Garlic Sauce

A slice of this pizza leaves you with an insane craving for it. You can serve slices with a tossed salad for a filling supper.
Prep Time and Cooking Time: 50 minutes| Serves: 8

Ingredients to use:

- 2 tbsp. butter, unsalted
- 2 tbsp. all-purpose flour
- 1 cup whole milk
- 1/4 tbsp. cayenne pepper, ground
- 3 heads garlic
- 1/4 tbsp. salt
- 1 cup of warm water
- 1 tbsp. honey
- 2 tbsp. olive oil
- 1-1/4 oz. active dry yeast
- 2-1/2 cup all-purpose flour
- 8 oz. mozzarella cheese
- 4 oz. fontina cheese, grated
- 1/2 cup Parmigiano- Reggiano cheese, finely grated
- 30 pieces tomatoes, sun-dried
- 2 tbsp. basil leaves, freshly chopped

Step-by-step Directions to Cook It:

1. Melt butter in a saucepan over medium heat and cook the all-purpose flour for 3 minutes.
2. Whisk in milk until thickened. Add pepper, garlic, and salt then simmer for 15 minutes on low heat to make the bechamel.
3. In a mixing bowl, mix warm water honey, and oil. Mix in the yeast, flour, and salt to the bowl. Knead until smooth. Let rest for 20 minutes.
4. Divide the pizza dough into half and roll it to make it fit the pizza rack.
5. Top with cheeses and tomatoes. Slide the pizza rack on position 5 and select the pizza setting on the Emeril Lagasse Power Air Fryer 360.
6. Set the temperature at 425°F for 20 minutes. Press start.
7. Repeat with the second pizza. Top the pizza with parsley, basil, and red pepper.

Nutritional value per serving:

Calories: 200kcal, Carbs: 34g Fat: 11g, Protein: 12g

Four Cheese Margherita Pizza

This four cheese Margherita is an amazing version of Italian classic pizza. The cheese brings out a rich flavor that is incredible and irresistible.

Prep Time and Cooking Time: 40 minutes| Serves: 8

Ingredients to use:

- 1/4 cup olive oil
- 1 tbsp. garlic, raw
- 1/2 tbsp. salt
- 8 Roma tomatoes
- 2 pizza crust
- 8 oz. mozzarella cheese
- 4 oz. fontina cheese
- 10 fresh basil
- 1/2 cup parmesan cheese, grated
- 1/2 cup feta cheese

Step-by-step Directions to Cook It:

1. Mix oil, garlic, and salt. Toss with tomatoes and let stand for 15 minutes.
2. Place the crust on the crisper tray and brush it with tomato marinade, then sprinkle mozzarella and fontina cheese.
3. Arrange the tomatoes on top then sprinkle basil, parmesan cheese, and feta cheese.
4. Slide the crisper tray on shelf position 2 of the Emeril Lagasse Power Air Fryer 360 and select the pizza setting. Set the temperature at 400°F for 15 minutes. Press start.
5. Cook until the cheese is golden brown and bubbly. Repeat the cycle with the remaining pizza.
6. Serve the pizza and enjoy it.

Nutritional value per serving:

Calories: 551kcal, Carbs: 54g Fat: 18g, Protein: 29g

Satay Chicken Pizza

A really amazing pizza that you will whip up even before you know it. It's also very delicious and a real crowd-pleaser.

Prep Time and Cooking Time: 27 minutes| Serves: 4

Ingredients to use:

- 1 tbsp. vegetable corn oil
- 2 chicken breasts
- 4 small pita bread
- 1 cup peanut sauce
- 1 bunch spring onions
- 4 slices provolone cheese

Step-by-step Directions to Cook It:

1. Heat oil in a nonstick skillet and sauté the chicken for 7 minutes.
2. Spoon peanut sauce on each pita bread the sprinkle the cooked chicken. Add scallions and a slice of cheese.
3. Place the pizza on a crisper tray lined with a cookie sheet.
4. Slide the crisper tray on shelf position 2 of the Emeril Lagasse Power Air Fryer 360.Select the pizza setting. Set the temperature at 400°F for 12 minutes. Press start.
5. Let the pizza stand for 2 minutes before cutting and serving.

Nutritional value per serving:

Calories: 391kcal, Carbs: 52g Fat: 18g, Protein: 7g

Black and White Pizza

The black and white pizza is quite fast to be prepared. It uses already prepared ingredients, making it simple to bring together.

Prep Time and Cooking Time: 30 minutes| Serves: 4

Ingredients to use:

- 1 tbsp. olive oil
- 1/2 garlic clove, raw
- 6 oz. chicken
- 2 prepared pizza crust
- 1 cup Di Giorno Alfredo sauce
- 6 Oz packed mozzarella cheese
- 1/2 cup beans
- 4 oz. jalapeno peppers
- 1 tbsp. dried parsley

Step-by-step Directions to Cook It:

1. Heat oil in a nonstick skillet over medium heat. Cook garlic until fragrant then add chicken and cook until heated through.
2. Spread Alfredo sauce on the pizza crust, then sprinkle some cheese.
3. Arrange chicken strips over the cheese then add black beans. Place peppers on top.
4. Add the remaining cheese then garnish with parsley. Place the pizza on a crisper tray of the Emeril Lagasse Power Air Fryer 360.
5. Slide the crisper tray on shelf position 2. Select the pizza setting. Set the temperature at 450°F for 15 minutes. Press start.
6. Cook until the crust is crispy and the cheese has melted.

Nutritional value per serving:

Calories: 731kcal, Carbs: 61g Fat: 38g, Protein: 41g

Bread Machine Bagels

These are delicious and quick bagels that you can make it at home. Use your favorite topping including poppy seeds.

Prep Time and Cooking Time: 50 minutes| Serves: 6

Ingredients to use:

- 1 cup of water
- 1-1/2 tbsp. salt
- 2 tbsp. sugar
- 3 cups wheat flour
- 2-1/4 tbsp. yeast
- 3 quarts water
- 3 tbsp. granulated sugar
- 1 tbsp. cornmeal
- 1 egg
- 3 tbsp. poppy seeds

Step-by-step Directions to Cook It:

1. Place water, sugar, salt, flour, and yeast in a bread machine. Select dough setting.
2. Let the dough rest on a floured surface.
3. Meanwhile, bring water to boil then stir with sugar. Cut dough into nine pieces and roll each into a ball.
4. Flatten and poke a hole on the ball using your hands. Cover the bagels and let rest for 10 minutes.
5. Sprinkle cornmeal on a baking sheet then transfer the bagels to boiling water. Let boil for 1 minute then drain them on a clean paper towel.
6. Arrange the bagels on a baking sheet then glaze them with egg and sprinkle poppy seeds.
7. Place the baking sheet on the pizza rack of the Emeril Lagasse Power Air Fryer 360 and Select the bake setting. Set the temperature at 375°F for 25 minutes. Press start.
8. The bagels should be well browned and cooked.

Nutritional value per serving:

Calories: 50kcal, Carbs: 9g Fat: 1.3g, Protein: 1.4g

Bagel and Cheese Bake

This is an amazing breakfast that resembles a casserole. You can make ahead of time and surprise your family in the morning with this amazing bake.
Prep Time and Cooking Time: 60 minutes| Serves: 12

Ingredients to use:

- 1/2 lb. pork
- 1/2 cup onions, raw
- 3 bagels
- 1 cup cheddar cheese
- 12 eggs
- 2 cups of milk, reduced fat
- 2 tbsp. parsley
- 1/4 tbsp. black pepper
- 1/2 cup parmesan cheese, grated

Step-by-step Directions to Cook It:

1. Cook bacon and onion in a nonstick skillet and cook over medium heat until well browned. Drain and set aside.
2. Slice the bagel into 6 slices then arrange them on a greased baking dish. Cover the bagels with bacon and onion mixture then top with cheese.
3. In a mixing bowl, whisk together eggs, milk, parsley, and pepper. Pour the egg mixture on the bagels and refrigerate overnight while covered.
4. Place the baking sheet on the pizza rack of the Emeril Lagasse Power Air Fryer 360 and select the bake setting. Set the temperature at 400°F for 30 minutes. Press start.
5. Sprinkle parmesan cheese and serve when warm. Enjoy.

Nutritional value per serving:

Calories: 249kcal, Carbs: 15g Fat: 13.5g, Protein: 17g

Chapter 10: Roasting Recipes

Dry-Roasted Chickpea

This is an amazing snack that is easy to make and can be customized to your preferences.
Prep Time and Cooking Time:54 minutes| Serves: 4

Ingredients to use:

- 15 oz. can chickpeas, canned
- 2 tbsp. olive oil
- 1/4 tbsp. salt
- 1 pinch black pepper

Step-by-step Directions to Cook It:

1. Spread chickpeas on a baking dish and pat them dry with a paper towel.
2. Place the baking dish on the pizza rack of the Emeril Lagasse Power Air Fryer 360 and Select the bake setting. Set the temperature at 425°F for 22 minutes. Press start.
3. Toss the chickpeas with oil, salt, and pepper then place back in the baking dish.
4. Continue to bake for 22 more minutes.

Nutritional value per serving:

Calories: 105kcal, Carbs: 16g Fat: 3.2g, Protein: 3.5g

Roasted Red Potatoes

If you are in love with deep-fried potatoes, these are a classic potatoes side dish that will amaze you.

Prep Time and Cooking Time: 1 hour 20 minutes| Serves: 6

Ingredients to use:

- 1/4 cup olive oil
- 2 lb. potatoes
- 5 fresh thyme
- 1 pinch salt
- 1 pinch cayenne pepper
- 1/2 sweet red bell pepper

Step-by-step Directions to Cook It:

1. Pour oil on a baking dish and place the potatoes in it. Toss the potatoes until well coated.
2. Sprinkle thyme, salt, pepper, and bell pepper.
3. Place the baking dish on the pizza rack of the Emeril Lagasse Power Air Fryer 360 and select the bake setting. Set the temperature at 400°F for 30 minutes. Press start.
4. When the cooking cycle is complete, toss the potatoes to turn over. Bake for an additional 20 minutes.
5. Turn the potatoes once more, and then bake for 15 more minutes or until evenly golden brown.
6. Toss once more and adjust seasonings. Transfer to a bowl and serve.

Nutritional value per serving:

Calories: 190kcal, Carbs: 25g Fat: 9.3g, Protein: 3g

Fondant Potatoes

This old school method of cooking potatoes provides a texture that is unlike anything else. Moist, delicious, tender, and creamy potatoes with crusty edges.

Prep Time and Cooking Time: 60 minutes| Serves: 6

Ingredients to use:

- 3 russet potatoes
- 2 tbsp. vegetable oil
- Salt and ground pepper
- 3 tbsp. butter
- 4 sprigs of thyme
- 1/2 cup chicken broth

Step-by-step Directions to Cook It:

1. Cut off the ends of potatoes and peel them from top to bottom to make them cylinders. Half the cylinders to make 6 cylinders.
2. Wash the potatoes in a bowl of water to remove starch. Pat dry with a paper towel.
3. Cook the potato in oil in an oven-safe skillet over medium heat until well browned. Season the potatoes with salt and pepper.
4. Use a paper towel held with tongs to blot out any oil on the potatoes from the skillet.
5. Add butter and thyme to the skillet. Paint butter on top of the potato using the thyme sprig. Cook until the butter forms and turns to pale tan color.
6. Season with salt and pepper if you like and add the chicken broth.
7. Transfer the skillet to the Emeril Lagasse Power Air Fryer 360 and place it on the pizza rack.
8. Select the roast setting. Set the temperature at 425°F for 30 minutes. Press start.
9. If the potatoes are tender, add more chicken broth and roast for 10 more minutes. Serve them with the remaining butter from the skillet.

Nutritional value per serving:

Calories: 239kcal, Carbs: 34g Fat: 11g, Protein: 4g

Roasted Cabbage

This delicious roasted cabbage is a perfect sandwich for your steak. It's easy and requires minimal time to put together.

Prep Time and Cooking Time: 40 minutes| Serves: 4

Ingredients to use:

- 2 tbsp. olive oil
- 1/2 head of cabbage
- 1 pinch garlic powder
- 1 pinch red pepper flakes
- 1 pinch salt
- 2 eaches lemon juice

Step-by-step Directions to Cook It:

1. Half the cabbage and brush each wedge with olive oil.
2. Brush olive oil on the cabbage then sprinkle garlic powder, pepper flakes, salt, and pepper.
3. Place the cabbage on the baking pan and place the baking pan on the pizza tray on shelf position 2.
4. Select the roast setting on the Emeril Lagasse Power Air Fryer 360 and set the temperature at 450°F for 15 minutes. Press start.
5. Squeeze lemon over cabbage and serve.

Nutritional value per serving:

Calories: 99kcal, Carbs: 9g Fat: 7g, Protein: 2g

Roasted Peanuts

This is a very easy recipe to make at home. Just throw the peanuts in the Emeril Lagasse Power Air Fryer 360 and wait for an hour undisrupted.

Prep Time and Cooking Time: 1 hour 10 minutes| Serves: 8

Ingredients to use:

- 1 lb. peanuts

Step-by-step Directions to Cook It:

1. Arrange the peanuts in a cookie sheet and place the cookie sheet on the pizza rack on shelf position 2.
2. Select the roast setting on the Emeril Lagasse Power Air Fryer 360 and set the temperature at 500°F for 1 hour. Press start.
3. Serve the peanuts warm.

Nutritional value per serving:

Calories: 321kcal, Carbs: 9g Fat: 28g, Protein: 15g

Roasted Cauliflower

This recipe can convert cauliflower avoiders to cauliflower lovers. The cauliflower comes out beautifully delicious.

Prep Time and Cooking Time:1 hour 15 minutes| Serves: 8

Ingredients to use:

- 1/4 cup butter, salted
- 1 tbsp. dill weed, resh
- 1 garlic clove
- 1 tbsp. lemon peel
- 1/2 tbsp. cumin
- 1/4 tbsp. salt
- 1/4 tbsp. black pepper
- 1 head cauliflower

Step-by-step Directions to Cook It:

1. Mix butter, dill weed, garlic clove, lemon zest, cumin, salt, and pepper.
2. Cut the cauliflower head so that it sits upright on the baking dish. Spread the butter mixture on it then cover the dish with foil.
3. Place the baking pan on the pizza rack on the Emeril Lagasse Power Air Fryer 360.
4. Select the roast setting. Set the temperature at 350°F for 1 hour 15 minutes. Press start.
5. Serve the cauliflower with the cauliflower juice.

Nutritional value per serving:

Calories: 77kcal, Carbs: 6g Fat: 6g, Protein: 3g

Roasted Chestnuts

These are perfect when served as a dessert with vanilla ice cream or eggnog. They can also be served as a snack.

Prep Time and Cooking Time:50 minutes| Serves: 6

Ingredients to use:

- 1 lb. chestnuts
- 1/4 cup butter, salted
- Salt
- Pinch cinnamon, ground

Step-by-step Directions to Cook It:

1. Cut a half-inch on each flat side of the nut and make sure the nut doesn't crack.
2. Place the nuts on a baking dish and place the dish on the pizza rack of the Emeril Lagasse Power Air Fryer 360.
3. Select the roast setting. Set the temperature at 375°F for 30 minutes. Press start.
4. When the cooking cycle is complete, place nuts on a skillet with butter and sauté over high heat.
5. Place the skillet in the oven and roast until the nuts are golden brown. Sprinkle with salt and cinnamon then serve.

Nutritional value per serving:

Calories: 217kcal, Carbs: 34g Fat: 9g, Protein: 1g

Chapter 11: Slow Cooking

Slow-cooked Mac and Cheese

Use your Emeril Lagasse Power Air Fryer 360 to make this delicious Mac and cheese and it will be a sure family favorite.

Prep Time and Cooking Time: 3 hours| Serves: 4

Ingredients to use:

- 1/2 lb. fontina cheese, grated
- 1/4 lb. provolone cheese, grated
- 1/4 lb. Parmigiano-Reggiano cheese, grated
- 3 tbsp. butter
- 12 oz. ditalini pasta
- 1-1/2 cup milk
- 8 oz. can evaporated milk
- 1 tbsp. salt
- 1/2 tbsp. black pepper, ground
- 2 tbsp. parsley, chopped
- 1/2 cup panko breadcrumbs

Step-by-step Directions to Cook It:

1. In a mixing bowl, mix all the cheese. Reserve 1/2 cup of the cheese mixture.
2. Grease the casserole dish with butter. Add butter, pasta, cheese mixture, milk, evaporated milk, salt, and pepper.
3. Spread parsley on top then add the reserved cheese mixture and finally the breadcrumbs.
4. Place the casserole dish on the pizza rack on shelf position 6 of the Emeril Lagasse Power Air Fryer 360.
5. Select the slow cook setting. Set the temperature at 275°F for 3 hours. Press start.
6. Serve and enjoy.

Nutritional value per serving:

Calories: 165kcal, Carbs: 31g Fat: 2.4g, Protein: 4g

Honey Garlic Chicken

Enjoy this amazing chicken recipe that takes a little time to prepare and it is a perfect weeknight dinner.

Prep Time and Cooking Time:4 hours| Serves: 6

Ingredients to use:

●4 chicken breasts, skinless and boneless
●1/2 cup honey
●1/2 cup soy sauce
●1/4 cup water
●2 tbsp. apple cider vinegar
●1 tbsp. garlic, minced

Step-by-step Directions to Cook It:

1. Line a casserole dish with parchment paper.
2. In a mixing bowl, mix honey, soy sauce, water, apple cider vinegar, and garlic.
3. Place the chicken breasts in the dish and pour the sauce over the chicken.
4. Place the casserole dish on the pizza rack on shelf position 6 of the Emeril Lagasse Power Air Fryer 360.
5. Select the slow cook setting. Set the temperature at 300°F for 6-7 hours. Press start.
6. Serve.

Nutritional value per serving:

Calories: 165kcal, Carbs: 31g Fat: 2.4g, Protein: 4g

Mashed Potatoes

These melt-in-the-mouths are a must-try. They are delicious and can be enjoyed by everyone including the kids.

Prep Time and Cooking Time: 3 hours| Serves: 8

Ingredients to use:

- 5 lb. red potatoes
- 1 tbsp. garlic
- 3 cubes of chicken stock
- 8 oz. sour cream
- 8 oz. cream cheese
- 1/2 cup butter, salted
- 1/4 tbsp. salt

Step-by-step Directions to Cook It:

1. In a pot over medium heat, add salted boiling water. Cook potatoes, garlic, and chicken stock until the potatoes are tender.
2. Drain the potato juice and preserve it.
3. In a mixing bowl, mash potatoes with sour cream, cream cheese, and reserved juice until your desired condition.
4. Transfer the mashed potato mixture into a casserole dish and place the dish on the pizza rack of the Emeril Lagasse Power Air Fryer 360.
5. Select the slow cook setting. Set the temperature at 250°F for 3 hours. Press start.
6. Season with salt and pepper before serving.

Nutritional value per serving:

Calories: 470kcal, Carbs: 48g Fat: 28g, Protein: 9g

Slow-Cooked Bread Pudding

This bread pudding is versatile. It can be served for breakfast, lunch, and dinner. It's an amazing dish that everyone will enjoy.

Prep Time and Cooking Time: 3 hours| Serves: 8

Ingredients to use:

- 8 cups bread, cubed
- 1 cup raisins
- 2 cups milk
- 4 eggs
- 1/4 cup butter, melted
- 1/4 cup white sugar
- 1/2 tbsp. vanilla extract
- 1/4 tbsp. nutmeg

Step-by-step Directions to Cook It:

1. Place the bread and raisins in a greased baking dish.
2. In a mixing bowl, whisk in milk, eggs, butter, sugar, vanilla, and nutmeg until well mixed.
3. Pour the mixture over the bread. Toss to coat well.
4. Place the baking dish on the pizza rack on shelf position 5 of the Emeril Lagasse Power Air Fryer 360.
5. Select the slow cook setting. Set the temperature at 2750°F for 3 hours. Press start.
6. Serve.

Nutritional value per serving:

Calories: 396kcal, Carbs: 58g Fat: 14g, Protein: 11g

Banana Foster

This banana foster is made by cooking ripe bananas in butter and rum sauce with coconut and walnuts. It's just amazing.

Prep Time and Cooking Time: 2 hours 10 minutes| Serves: 4

Ingredients to use:

- 4 bananas
- 4 tbsp. butter, salted
- 1 cup brown sugar
- 1/4 cup rum
- 1 tbsp. vanilla extract
- 1/2 tbsp. cinnamon, ground
- 1/4 cups coconut meat, unsweetened and dried
- 1/4 cups walnuts

Step-by-step Directions to Cook It:

1. Layer the bananas at the bottom of the baking dish.
2. In a mixing bowl, mix butter, sugar, rum, vanilla, and cinnamon. Pour the mixture over the bananas.
3. Place the baking dish over the pizza rack on shelf position 6 of Emeril Lagasse Power Air Fryer 360 and select the slow cook setting. Set the temperature at 275°F for 2 hours. Press start.
4. During the last 30 minutes of cooking, top the bananas with coconut meat and walnuts.
5. Enjoy.

Nutritional value per serving:

Calories: 539kcal, Carbs: 84g Fat: 21g, Protein: 3g

Beef Stew

This beef stew is amazingly delicious. It needs to be cooked slowly to allow the blending of flavors, it's the best stew to cook at lunch or dinner times.

Prep Time and Cooking Time:10 hours 10 minutes| Serves: 8

Ingredients to use:

- 2 lb. beef meat, cut into cubes
- 1/4 cup all-purpose flour
- 1/2 tbsp. salt
- 1/2 tbsp. black pepper, ground
- 1 garlic clove
- 1 bay leaf
- 1 tbsp. paprika
- 1 tbsp. Worcestershire sauce
- 1 onion, chopped
- 1-1/2 cup beef broth
- 3 potatoes, diced
- 4 carrots, sliced
- 1 celery stalk

Step-by-step Directions to Cook It:

1. Place the meat in a deep casserole dish.
2. In a mixing bowl, mix all other ingredients and pour over the meat.
3. Place the dish on a pizza rack of the Emeril Lagasse Power Air Fryer 360 and select the slow cook function for 10 hours at 300°F.
4. Serve the beef stew with a side dish of choice.

Nutritional value per serving:

Calories: 576kcal, Carbs: 30g Fat: 30g, Protein: 44g

Tapioca Pudding

This is a classy pudding that is very easy but needs to be slow-cooked. You do not need to soak the tapioca pearls ahead of time.

Prep Time and Cooking Time: 3 hours 5 minutes| Serves: 8

Ingredients to use:

●4 cups milk
●2/3 cup granulated sugar
●1/2 cup Bascom Imported Gran
●2 eggs

Step-by-step Directions to Cook It:

1. Mix milk, sugar, tapioca, and eggs in a mixing bowl then pour over the mixture in a casserole dish.
2. Place the dish on a pizza rack of the Emeril Lagasse Power Air Fryer 360 and select the slow cook setting. Set the temperature at 250°F for 3 hours. Press start.
3. Stir occasionally during the cooking cycle.
4. Serve the pudding when warm.

Nutritional value per serving:

Calories: 190kcal, Carbs: 30g Fat: 5g, Protein: 7g

Chapter 12: Snacks And Desserts

Lemon Poppy Seed Cake

This is an amazing poppy seed cake to serve your family, friends coming over , or gatherings as a snack.

Prep Time and Cooking Time:1 hour 30 minutes| Serves: 8

Ingredients to use:

- 3 tbsp. coconut milk
- 3 eggs
- 2 tbsp. vanilla extract
- 1-1/2 cup cake flour, sifted
- 3/4 cup sugar
- 3/4 tbsp. baking soda
- 1/4 tbsp. salt
- 12 tbsp. butter, softened
- 3 tbsp. poppy seeds
- 1 tbsp. lemon zest

Step-by-step Directions to Cook It:

1. In a mixing bowl, mix milk, eggs, and vanilla until well mixed.
2. In a separate mixing bowl, mix the dry ingredients.
3. Add butter and half the coconut milk mixture to the dry ingredients. Use a hand mixer to mix until well combined.
4. Scrape down the sides and add the remaining coconut milk mixture alongside the poppy seeds and lemon zest.
5. Scoop the batter into the loaf pan and place the loaf pan on the pizza rack of the Emeril Lagasse Air fryer 360.
6. Select the bake setting then set the temperature at 360°F for 1 hour 15 minutes. Press start.
7. Cover the cake with foil when it starts to brown before it's fully cooked.

Nutritional value per serving:

Calories: 165kcal, Carbs: 31g Fat: 2.4g, Protein: 4g

Coffee Cake

This is a tender moist cake that you and your family will love. It's easy to put together and gluten-free.

Prep Time and Cooking Time: 30 minutes| Serves: 12

Ingredients to use:

- 1/2 cup butter, unsalted
- 1 cup sugar
- 2 tbsp. vanilla extract
- 2 eggs
- 1/2 cup sour cream
- 1/2 cup buttermilk
- 2 cups all-purpose flour
- 1 tbsp. baking powder
- 1/2 tbsp. salt
- 1 cup all-purpose baking flour, gluten-free
- 1/2 cup brown sugar
- 2 tbsp. granulated sugar
- 1/8 tbsp. salt
- 2 tbsp. cinnamon
- 1/3 cup unsalted butter

Step-by-step Directions to Cook It:

1. Spray a baking pan with cooking spray.
2. In a mixing bowl, add butter, sugar, and vanilla. Mix them using a hand mixer until smooth.
3. Add eggs, sour cream, and buttermilk and continue to beat until fluffy.
4. Sift flour, baking powder, and salt into the bowl. Mix at low speed while scraping down the sides with a rubber spatula.
5. Pour batter on the baking pan and use the spatula to smooth the top.
6. Add flour, sugar, granulated sugar, cinnamon, and salt in a mixing bowl. Mix with a fork. Drizzle melted butter and continue mixing until the mixture forms crumbs.
7. Sprinkle the crumbs on the cake batter. Place the cake pan on the pizza rack of the Emeril Lagasse Power Air Fryer 360.
8. Select the bake setting. Set the temperature at 350°F for 45 minutes. Press start.
9. Insert a toothpick to check if the cake is well cooked. Serve when it has cooled.

Nutritional value per serving:

Calories: 260kcal, Carbs: 29g Fat: 16g, Protein: 2g

Bacon-Wrapped Asparagus

This is a classy and amazing snack idea that is a real crowd-pleaser. You can make them in large batches if you want to serve a large crowd.

Prep Time and Cooking Time: 30 minutes| Serves: 2

Ingredients to use:

- 10 asparagus
- 1/8 black pepper
- 5 bacon strips

Step-by-step Directions to Cook It:

1. Place the asparagus on a waxed paper then cut the bacon into halves.
2. Wrap a bacon piece around each asparagus then fix with a toothpick. Sprinkle black pepper and make sure it's evenly coated.
3. Place the asparagus on the crisper tray then slide it on shell position 4 of the Emeril Lagasse Power Air Fryer 360.
4. Select the air fry setting and set the temperature at 400°F for 15 minutes. Press start.
5. The bacon should be crispy. Remove the toothpick before serving. Enjoy.

Nutritional value per serving:

Calories: 109kcal, Carbs: 4g Fat: 8g, Protein: 7g

Country Apple Dumpling

Do you know that fresh apples, crescent dough, and citrus soda can make an awesome dessert that you will love?

Prep Time and Cooking Time: 1 hour 5 minutes| Serves: 16

Ingredients to use:

- 2 Granny Smith apple, peeled
- 10 oz. cans crescent roll dough
- 1 cup butter, salted
- 1-1/2 cup sugar, granulated
- 1 tbsp. cinnamon, ground
- 12 oz. bottle mountain dew soda pop PCO

Step-by-step Directions to Cook It:

1. Slice each apple into 8 pieces and set aside.
2. Separate roll dough into triangles then wrap each piece of apple with the dough starting from the bottom. Seal by pinching using your hands and place in a baking dish.
3. Meanwhile, melt butter in a saucepan over medium heat. Stir with cinnamon and sugar.
4. Pour over the dumpling followed by the mountain dew.
5. Place the baking dish on the pizza rack of the Emeril Lagasse Power Air Fryer 360.
6. Select the bake setting then set the temperature at 350°F for 45 minutes. Press start.
7. Cook until golden brown. Serve.

Nutritional value per serving:

Calories: 333kcal, Carbs: 3g Fat: 19g, Protein: 3g

Cinnamon Sweet Potato Chips

Are you a potato chips lover? These are a great alternative to potato chips. They are perfect for game day or movie night.

Prep Time and Cooking Time: 30 minutes| Serves: 4

Ingredients to use:

- 2 eaches sweet potato, raw
- 1 tbsp. butter, salted
- 1/2 tbsp. salt
- 2 tbsp. brown sugar
- 1/2 tbsp. cinnamon, ground

Step-by-step Directions to Cook It:

1. Arrange the sweet potato slices in a single layer on a baking sheet.
2. In a mixing bowl, mix butter, salt, sugar, and cinnamon. Brush the mixture on the sweet potatoes slices.
3. Place the baking sheet on the pizza rack and select the bake setting. Set the temperature at 400°F for 25 minutes. Press start.
4. Cook until crispy. Serve immediately.

Nutritional value per serving:

Calories: 157kcal, Carbs: 31g Fat: 2.4g, Protein: 2.3g

Baked Carrots Chips

Make these crunchy chips and eat to your satisfaction without ruining your diet. It's a low calorie snack that you will love.
Prep Time and Cooking Time: 40 minutes| Serves: 8

Ingredients to use:

- 2 lb. carrots
- 1/4 cup olive oil
- 1 tbsp. salt
- 1 tbsp. cumin, ground
- 1 tbsp. cinnamon, ground

Step-by-step Directions to Cook It:

1. Line a baking sheet with parchment paper. Set aside.
2. Trim the top of the carrots then slice the carrots into thin slices.
3. Place the carrot slices in a mixing bowl, and add olive oil, salt, cumin, and cinnamon. Mix until well coated.
4. Lay the slices on the baking sheet and place the baking sheet on the pizza rack of the Emeril Lagasse Power Air Fryer 360.
5. Select the bake setting. Set the temperature at 425°F for 15 minutes. Press start.
6. The chips should be golden brown and the edges having curved.

Nutritional value per serving:

Calories: 107kcal, Carbs: 11g Fat: 7g, Protein: 1g

CPSIA information can be obtained
at www.ICGtesting.com
Printed in the USA
LVHW102144210121
677101LV00008BB/34

9 781922 547231